AF348330

Cliges
A Romance

by

Chretien de Troyes

Cliges
A Romance
by Chretien de Troyes

Copyright © 2023

All Rights reserved.

No part of this publication may be reproduced, stored in a retrieval system, or transmitted in any form or by any means, electronic, mechanical, photocopying or Otherwise, without the written permission of the publisher.
The author/editor asserts the moral right to be identified as the author/editor of this work.

ISBN: 978-93-60461-52-2

Published by

DOUBLE 9 BOOKS

2/13-B, Ansari Road
Daryaganj, New Delhi – 110002
info@double9books.com
www.double9books.com
Tel. 011-40042856

This book is under public domain

ABOUT THE AUTHOR

Chrétien de Troyes was a French author and soldier who lived from 1160 to 1191. He was famous for writing about Arthurian characters like Gawain, Lancelot, Perceval, and the Holy Grail. Some of the most famous works of medieval writing are Chrétien's chivalric romances, such as Erec and Enide, Lancelot, Perceval and Yvain, and others. People see his use of framework, especially in Yvain, as a step toward the modern novel. We don't know much about his life, but he seems to have been from Troyes or very close to it. Gaston Paris thought he might have been a herald-at-arms at the court of his patroness Marie of France, Countess of Champagne, from 1160 to 1172. Marie was the daughter of King Louis VII and Eleanor of Aquitaine and married Count Henry I of Champagne in 1164. He then worked for Philippe d'Alsace, Count of Flanders, at his court. According to Urban T. Holmes III, Chrétien's name, which means "Christian from Troyes" in English, could be the stage name of a Jewish person who converted to Christianity and was also known as Crestien li Gois.

CONTENTS

INTRODUCTION

IT is six hundred and fifty years since Chretien de Troyes wrote his Cliges. And yet he is wonderfully near us, whereas he is separated by a great gulf from the rude trouveres of the Chansons de Gestes and from the Anglo-Saxon Chronicle, which was still dragging out its weary length in his early days. Chretien is as refined, as civilised, as composite as we are ourselves; his ladies are as full of whims, impulses, sudden reserves, self-debate as M. Paul Bourget's heroines; while the problems of conscience and of emotion which confront them are as complex as those presented on the modern stage. Indeed, there is no break between the Breton romance and the psychological-analytical novel of our own day.

Whence comes this amazing modernity and complexity? From many sources:—Provencal love-lore, Oriental subtlety, and Celtic mysticism—all blended by that marvellous dexterity, style, malice, and measure which are so utterly French that English has no adequate words for them. We said "Celtic mysticism," but there is something else about Chretien which is also Celtic, though very far from being "mystic". We talk a great deal nowadays about Celtic melancholy, Celtic dreaminess, Celtic "other-worldliness"; and we forget the qualities that made Caesar's Gauls, St. Paul's Galatians, so different from the grave and steadfast Romans—that loud Gaulois that has made the Parisian the typical Frenchman. A different being, this modern Athenian, from the mystic Irish peasant we see in the poetic modern Irish drama!—and yet both are Celts.

Not much "other-worldliness" about Chretien. He is as positive as any man can be. His is not of the world of Saint Louis, of the Crusaders, of the Cathedral-builders. In Cliges there is no religious atmosphere at all. We hear scarcely anything of Mass, of bishops, of convents. When he mentions Tierce or Prime, it is merely to tell us the hour at which something happened—and this something is never a religious service. There is nothing behind the glamour of arms and love, except for the cas de conscience presented by the lovers. Nothing but names and framework are Celtic; the spirit, with its refinements and its hair-splitting, is Provencal. But what a brilliant whole! what art! what measure! Our thoughts turn to the gifted women of the age—as subtle, as interesting, and as unscrupulous as the women of the

Renaissance—to Eleanor of Aquitaine, a reigning princess, a troubadour, a Crusader, the wife of two kings, the mother of two kings, to the last, intriguing and pulling the strings of political power—"An Ate, stirring him [King John] to blood and strife."

The twelfth century was an age in which women had full scope—in which the Empress Maud herself took the field against her foe, in which Stephen's queen seized a fortress, in which a wife could move her husband to war or to peace, in which a Marie of Champagne (Eleanor's daughter) could set the tone of great poets and choose their subjects.

If, then, this woman-worship, this complexity of love, this self-debating, first comes into literature with Chretien de Troyes, and is still with us, no more interesting work exists than his earliest masterpiece, Cliges. The delicate and reticent Soredamors; the courteous and lovable, Guinevere; the proud and passionate Fenice, who will not sacrifice her fair fame and chastity; the sorceress Thessala, ancestress of Juliet's nurse—these form a gallery of portraits unprecedented in literature.

The translator takes this opportunity of thanking Mr. B. J. Hayes, M.A., of St. John's College, Cambridge, for occasional help, and also for kindly reading the proofs.

THE clerk who wrote the tale of Erec and Enid, and translated the Commandments of Ovid and the Art of Love, and composed the Bite of the Shoulder, and sang of King Mark and of the blonde Iseult, and of the metamorphosis of the Hoopoe and of the Swallow and of the Nightingale, is now beginning a new tale of a youth who was in Greece of the lineage of King Arthur. But before I tell you anything of him, you shall hear his father's life—whence he was and of what lineage. So valiant was he and of such proud spirit, that to win worth and praise he went from Greece to England, which was then called Britain. We find this story that I desire to tell and to relate to you, recorded in one of the books of the library of my lord Saint Peter at Beauvais. Thence was taken the tale from which Chretien framed this romance. The book, which truthfully bears witness to the story, is very ancient; for this reason it is all the more to be believed. From the books which we possess, we know the deeds of the ancients and of the world which aforetime was. This our books have taught us: that Greece had the first renown in chivalry and in learning. Then came chivalry to Rome, and the heyday of learning, which now is come into France. God grant that she be maintained there; and that her home there please her so much that never may depart from France the honour which has there taken up its abode. God had lent that glory to others; but no man talks any longer either more or less about Greeks and Romans; talk of them has ceased, and the bright glow is extinct.

Chretien begins his tale—as the story relates to us—which tells of an emperor mighty in wealth and honour, who ruled Greece and Constantinople. There was a very noble empress by whom the emperor had two children. But the first was of such an age before the other was born, that if he had willed he might have become a knight and held all the empire. The first was named Alexander; the younger was called Alis. The father too had for name Alexander; and the mother had for name Tantalis. I will straight-away leave speaking of the empress Tantalis, of the emperor, and of Alis. I will speak to you of Alexander, who was so great-hearted and proud that he did not stoop to become a knight in his own realm. He had heard mention made of King Arthur, who was reigning at that time; and of the barons which he ever maintained in his retinue wherefore his Court was feared and famed throughout the world. Howe'er the end may fall out for him, and whate'er may come of it for the lad, there is nought that will hold him from his yearning to go to Britain; but it is meet that he take leave of his father before he goes to Britain or to Cornwall. Alexander the fair, the valiant, goes to speak to the emperor in order to ask permission and to take his leave. Now will he tell him what is his vow, and what he would fain do and take in hand. "Fair sire, that I may be schooled in honour and win worth and renown, a boon," quoth he, "I venture to crave of you—a boon that I would have you give me; never defer it now for me if you are destined to grant it." The emperor had no thought of being vexed for that, either much or little; he is bound to desire and to covet honour for his son above aught else. He would deem himself to be acting well—would deem? ay, and he would be so acting—if he increased his son's honour. "Fair son," quoth he, "I grant you your good pleasure, and tell me what you would have me give you." Now the lad has done his work well; and right glad was he of it when is granted him the boon that he so longed to have. "Sire," quoth he, "would you know what you have promised me? I wish to have in great store of your gold and of your silver and comrades from your retinue such as I shall will to choose; for I wish to go forth from your empire, and I shall go to offer my service to the king who reigns over Britain, that he may dub me knight. Never, indeed, on any day as long as I live shall I wear visor on my face or helm on my head, I warrant you, till King Arthur gird on my sword if he deign to do it; for I will receive arms of no other." The emperor without more ado replies: "Fair son, in God's name, say not so. This land and mighty are diverse and contrary. And that man is a slave. Constantinople is wholly yours. You must not hold me a niggard when I would fain give you so fair a boon. Soon will I have you crowned; and a knight shall you be to-morrow. All Greece shall be in your hand; and you shall receive from your barons— as indeed you ought to receive—their oaths and homage. He who refuses this is no wise man."

The lad hears the promise—namely, that his father will dub him knight on the morrow after Mass—but says that he will prove himself coward or hero in another land than his own. "If you will grant my boon in that matter in which I have asked you; then give me fur both grey and of divers colour and good steeds and silken attire; for before I am knight I will fain serve King Arthur. Not yet have I so great valour that I can bear arms. None by entreaty or by fair words could persuade me not to go into the foreign land to see the king and his barons, whose renown for courtesy and for prowess is so great. Many high men through their idleness lose great praise that they might have if they wandered o'er the world. Repose and praise agree all together, as it seems to me; for a man of might who is ever resting in no wise becomes famous. Prowess is a burden to a cowardly man; and cowardice is a burden to the brave; thus the twain to his possessions who is ever heaping them up and increasing them. Fair sire, as long as I am allowed to win renown, if I can avail so much, I will give my pains and diligence to it."

At this, without doubt, the emperor feels joy and anxiety—joy has he; for that he perceives that his son aims at valiant deeds; and anxiety on the other hand, for that he is leaving him. But because of the promise that he has made him it behoves him to grant his boon whatever anxiety he feel about it; for an emperor must not lie. "Fair son," quoth he, "I ought not to fail to do your pleasure, since I see that you aspire to honour. You may take from my treasury two barques full of gold and silver; but take care that you be very generous and courteous and well-bred." Now is the youth right glad; for his father promises him so much that he puts his treasure at his free disposal and exhorts and commands him to give and to spend liberally; and also he tells him the reason wherefore: "Fair son," quoth he, "believe me in this; that open-handedness is the lady and queen who illumines all virtues; and it is not a whit difficult to prove this. In what place could one find a man, however mighty and magnificent he be, that is not blamed if he be a niggard; or any man, however ill-reputed he be, whom liberality does not render praised? Liberality of itself makes a man of honour—which neither high Rank, nor courtesy, nor knowledge, nor noble birth, nor wealth, nor strength, nor chivalry, nor courage, nor lordship, nor beauty, nor any other thing, can do. But just as the rose is fairer than any other flower when she buddeth fresh and new; so where liberality comes she holds herself above all virtues, and she multiplies five hundredfold the virtues that she finds in an honourable man who proves his worth. There is so much to say about liberality that I could not tell the half of it." Well has the lad succeeded in whatsoever he has requested and asked; for his father has found for him all that his desire conceived. Exceeding sorrowful was the empress when she heard of the road which her son must needs follow; but whoever has grief and anxiety thereof, or whoever deems his conduct but folly, or blames and dissuades him, the youth as quickly as he could bade his ships be got ready; for he had no wish to stay longer in his own country. The ships were loaded that night by his command with wine with meat and with biscuits.

The ships are loaded in the harbour and on the morrow with great joyance came Alexander to the sandy shore; and with him his comrades who were fain of the journey. The emperor convoys him and the empress who was sad at heart. In the harbour they find the mariners in the ships beside the cliff. The sea was peaceful and smooth the wind gentle and the air serene. Alexander first of all, when he had parted from his father and on taking leave of the empress whose heart was sad within her, enters from the boat into the ship and his comrades with him. Four, three, and two, they simultaneously strive to enter without delay. Full soon was the sail spread and the anchor of the barque weighed. Those on land, who were sore at heart for the lads whom they see departing, follow them with their eyes' ken as far as they can; and so that they may watch them the better and the further, they go off and climb together a high peak by the shore. Thence they watch their sorrow as far as they can see them. They gaze at their own sorrow in sooth; for great is their sorrow for the lads: may God lead them to port without disaster and without peril!

They were at sea all April and part of May. Without great peril and without alarm they made land above Southampton. One day 'twixt Nones and Vespers they cast anchor and have made the port. The youths, who had never previously learned to suffer discomfort or pain, had stayed on the sea which was not wholesome for them so long that all are pale and all the strongest and most healthy are weakened and nerveless. And, nevertheless, they show great joy; for that they have escaped from the sea and come hither where they would be. And because they were suffering greatly, they lie that night above Southampton and show great joy and let ask and inquire whether the king is in England. They are told that he is at Winchester; and that they can be there full soon if they will depart with morning provided that they keep to the right way. This news pleases them well; and on the morrow, when the day is born, the lads wake up with morning and equip and prepare themselves. And when they were equipped they have turned from above Southampton and have kept to the right way till they have reached Winchester where the king was tarrying. Before Prime the Greeks had come to Court. They dismount at the foot of the steps, the squires and the horses stayed in the court below; and the youths ascend to the presence of the best king that ever was or ever may be in the world. And when the king sees them come, they please and delight him much; but ere they had come before him, they throw off the cloaks from their necks that they might not be taken for clowns. Thus all having thrown off their cloaks have come before the king. And the barons one and all keep silence; for the youths please them mightily for that they see them fair and comely. Never do they dream that they are all sons of counts or of a king; yet truly so they were, and they were in the flower of their youth, comely and well set up in body; and the robes that they wore were of one cloth and one cut, of one appearance and one colour. Twelve were they without their lord of whom I will tell you this much without more ado; that none was better than he; but without arrogance and yet unabashed he stood with his mantle off before the king, and was very fair and well shaped. He has kneeled down before him, and all the others from courtesy, kneel beside their lord.

Alexander, whose tongue was sharpened to speak well and wisely, greets the king. "King," quoth he, "if renown lie not concerning you since God made the first man, no king with faith in God was born so powerful as you. King, the report that is in men's mouths has brought me to your Court to serve and honour you, and if my service is pleasing I will stay till I be a new-made knight at your hand, not at that of another. For never shall I be dubbed knight if I be not so by you. If my service so please you that you will to make me a knight, keep me, gracious king, and my comrades who are here." Straightway the king replies: "Friend," quoth he, "I reject not a whit either you or your company; but ye are all right welcome; for ye have the air, I well think it, of being sons of men of high rank. Whence are ye?" "We are from Greece." "From Greece?" "Truly are we." "Who is thy father?" "Faith, sire, the emperor." "And what is thy name, fair friend?" "Alexander was the name given me when I received salt and chrism and Christianity and baptism." "Alexander, fair dear friend, I keep you right willingly; and much does it please and joy me, for you have done me exceeding great honour in that you are come to my Court. It is my good pleasure that you be honoured here as a noble warrior, wise and gentle. Too long have you been on your knees: rise, I bid you, and henceforth be free of my Court and of me; for you have arrived at a good haven."

Forthwith the Greeks rise. Blithe are they for that the king has thus courteously kept them. Alexander is welcome; for there is no lack of aught that he wishes nor is there any baron in the Court so high that he does not speak him fair and welcome him. For he is not foolish nor boastful nor doth he vaunt his noble birth. He makes himself known to Sir Gawain and to the others one by one. He makes himself much loved by each; even Sir Gawain loves him so much that he hails him as friend and comrade. The Greeks had taken in the town at the house of a citizen the best lodging that they could find. Alexander had brought great possessions from Constantinople: he will desire above aught else to follow diligently the emperor's advice and counsel—namely, that he should have his heart wide-awake to give and to spend liberally. He gives great diligence and pains thereto. He lives well at his lodging and gives and spends liberally as it beseems his wealth, and as his heart counsels him. The whole Court marvels whence his store is taken; for he gives to all horses of great price which he had brought from his land. So much trouble has Alexander given himself, and so much has he prevailed by his fair service, that the king loves and esteems him dearly as well the barons and the queen.

At that point of time King Arthur desired to pass over into Brittany. He bids all his barons assemble in order to seek Counsel, and ask them to whom till he return he can entrust England, who may keep and maintain it in peace. By the Council it was with one consent entrusted, as I think, to Count Engres of Windsor; for till then they deemed no baron more loyal in all the king's land. When this man had the land in his power, King Arthur and the queen and her ladies set out on the morrow. In Brittany folk hear tell that the king and his barons are coming: the Bretons rejoice greatly thereat.

Into the ship in which the king crossed entered neither youth nor maiden save Alexander alone; and the queen of a truth brought thither

Soredamors, a lady who scorned Love. Never had she heard tell of a man whom she could deign to love however much beauty prowess dominion or high rank he had. And yet the damsel was so winsome and fair that she might well have known Love if it had pleased her to turn her mind to it; but never had she willed to bend her mind thereto. Now will Love make her sorrowful; and Love thinks to avenge himself right well for the great pride and resistance which she has always shown to him. Right well has Love aimed; for he has stricken her in the heart with his arrow. Oft she grows pale; oft the beads of sweat break out, and in spite of herself she must love. Scarce can she refrain from looking towards Alexander; but she must needs guard herself against my Lord Gawain her brother. Dearly does she buy and pay for her great pride and her disdain. Love has heated for her a bath which mightily inflames and enkindles her. Now is he kind to her, now cruel; now she wants him, and now she rejects him. She accuses her eyes of treachery and says: "Eyes, you have betrayed me. Through you has my heart which was wont to be faithful conceived hatred for me. Now does what I see bring grief. Grief? Nay, in truth, but rather pleasure. And if I see aught that grieves me, still have I not my eyes under my own sway? My strength must indeed have failed me; and I must esteem myself but lightly if I cannot control my eyes and make them look elsewhere. By so doing I shall be able to guard myself right well from Love, who wishes to be my master. What the eye sees not the heart does not lament. If I do not see him there will be no pain. He does not entreat or seek me: if he had loved me he would have sought me. And since he neither loves nor esteems me, shall I love him if he loves me not? If his beauty draws my eyes, and my eyes obey the spell, shall I for that say I love him? Nay, for that would be a lie. By drawing my eyes he has done me no wrong of which I can complain; and I can bring no charge at all against him. One cannot love with the eyes. And what wrong, then, have my eyes done to me if they gaze on what I will to look at? What fault and wrong do they commit? Ought I to blame them? Nay. Whom, then? Myself, who have them in my keeping? My eye looks on nought unless it pleases and delights my heart. My heart could not wish for aught that would make me sorrowful. It is my heart's will that makes me sorrow. Sorrow? Faith, then, am I mad? since through my heart I desire that which makes me mad. I ought, indeed, if I can to rid myself of a will whence grief may come to me. If I can? Fool, what have I said? Then were I weak indeed if I had no power over myself. Does Love think to put me in the way which is wont to mislead other folk? Thus may he lead others; but I am not his at all. Never shall I be so; never was I so; never shall I desire his further acquaintance." Thus she disputes with herself, one hour loves and another hates. She is in such doubt that she does not know which side to take. She thinks she is defending herself against Love; but she is in no need of defence. God! Why does she not know that the thoughts of Alexander, on his side, are directed towards her? Love deals out to them impartially such a portion as is meet for each. He gives to them many a reason and ground that the one should love and desire the other. This love would have been loyal and right if the one had known what was the will of the other; but he does not know what she desires, nor she, for what he is lamenting. The queen watches them and sees the one and the other often lose colour and grow pale and sigh and shudder; but she knows not why they do it unless it be on account of the sea on which they are sailing. Perhaps, indeed, she would have perceived it if the sea had not misled her; but it is the sea which baffles and deceives her so that amid the sea-sickness she sees not the heart-sickness. For they are at sea, and heart-sickness is the cause of their plight, and heart-bitterness is the cause of the malady that grips them; but of these three the queen can only blame the sea; for heart-sickness and heart-bitterness lay the blame on the sea-sickness; and because of the third the two who are guilty get off scot-free. He who is guiltless of fault or wrong often pays dear for the sin of another. Thus the queen violently accuses the sea and blames it; but wrongly is the blame laid on the sea, for the sea has done therein no wrong. Much sorrow has Soredamors borne ere the ship has come to port. The king's coming is noised abroad; for the Bretons had great joy thereof and served him right willingly as their lawful lord. I seek not to speak more at length of King Arthur at this time: rather shall ye hear me tell how Love torments the two lovers against whom he has taken the field.

Alexander loves and desires her who is sighing for his love; but he knows not, and will not know aught of this until he shall have suffered many an ill and many a grief. For love of her he serves the queen and the ladies of her chamber; but he does not dare to speak to or address her who is most in his mind. If she had dared to maintain against him the right which she thinks is hers in the matter, willingly would he have told him of it; but she neither dares nor ought to do so. And the fact that the one sees the other, and that they dare not speak or act, turns to great adversity for them; and love grows thereby and burns. But it is the custom of all lovers that they willingly feed their eyes on looks if they can do no better, and think that because the source whence their love buds and grows delights them therefore it must help their case, whereas it injures them: just as the man who approaches and comes close to the fire burns himself more than the man who draws back from it. Their love grows and increases continually; but the one feels shame before the other; and each conceals and hides this love so that neither flame nor smoke is seen from the gleed beneath the ashes. But the heat is none the less for that; rather the heat lasts longer below the gleed than above it. Both the lovers are in very great anguish; for in order that their complaint may not be known or perceived, each must deceive all men by false pretence; but in the night great is the plaint which each makes in solitude.

First will I tell you of Alexander: how he complains and laments. Love brings before his mind the lady for whose sake he feels such Sorrow; for she has robbed him of his heart, and will not let him rest in his bed; so much it delights him to recall the beauty and the mien of her as to whom he dare not hope that ever joy of her may fall to his lot. "I may hold myself a fool," quoth he. "A fool? Truly am I a fool, since I do not dare to say what I think; for quickly would it turn to my bane. I have set my thought on folly. Then is it not better for me to meditate in silence than to get myself dubbed a fool? Never shall my desire be known. And shall I hide the cause of my grief, and not dare to seek help or succour for my sorrows? He who is conscious of weakness is a fool if he does not seek that by which he may have health if he can find it anywhere; but many a one thinks to gain his own advantage and to win what he desires, who pursues that whereof he sorrows later. And why should he go to seek advice when he does not expect to find health? That were a vain toil! I feel my own ill so heavy a burden that never shall I find healing for it by medicine or by potion or by herb or by root. There is not a remedy for every ill: mine is so rooted that it cannot be cured. Cannot? Methinks I have lied. As soon as I first felt this evil, if I had dared to reveal and to tell it, I could have spoken to a leech, who could have helped me in the whole matter; but it is very grievous for me to speak out. Perhaps they would not deign to listen and would refuse to accept a fee. No wonder is it then if I am dismayed, for I have a great ill; and yet I do not know what ill it is which sways me nor do I know whence comes this pain. I do not know? Yes, indeed, I think I know; Love makes me feel this evil. How? Does Love, then, know how to do evil? Is he not kind and debonair? I thought that there would have been nought in Love which was not good; but I have found him very malicious. He who has not put him to the test knows not with what games Love meddles. He is a fool who goes to meet him; for always he wishes to burden his subjects. Faith! his game is not at all a good one. It is ill playing with him; for his sport will cause me sorrow. What shall I do, then? Shall I draw back I think that this would be the act of a wise man; but I cannot tell how to set about it. If Love chastises and threatens in order to teach me his lesson, ought I to disdain my master? He who despises his master is a fool. Needs must I store up in my mind Love's lesson for soon can great good come of it. But he buffets me greatly: that sets me in alarm! True, neither blow nor wound is visible and yet dost thou complain? Then art thou not wrong? Nay, indeed, for he has wounded me so sore that he has winged his arrow even to my heart; and not yet has he drawn it out again.

How then has he struck his dart into thy body when no wound appears without? This shalt thou tell me; I would fain know it. In what member has he struck thee? Through the eye. Through the eye? And yet he has not put out thine eye? He has done me no hurt in the eye; but he wounds me sorely at the heart. Now speak reason to me: how has the dart passed through thine eye in such wise that the eye is not wounded or bruised by it? If the dart enter through the midst of the eye, why does my heart suffer pain in my body? Why does not my eye also feel the pain, since it receives the first blow? That can I well explain. The eye has no care to understand aught nor can it do anything in the matter in any way; but the eye is the mirror to the heart, and through this mirror passes the fire by which the heart is kindled; yet so that it neither wounds nor braises it. Then is not the heart placed in the body like the lighted candle which is put inside the lantern? If you take the candle out, never will any light issue thence; but as long as the candle lasts the lantern is not dark; and the flame which shines through neither harms nor injures it. Likewise is it with regard to a window: never will it be so strong and so whole but that the ray of the sun may pass through it without hurting it in any way; and the glass will never be so clear that one will see any better for its brightness if another brightness does not strike upon it. Know that it is the same with the eyes as with the glass and the lantern; for the light penetrates into the eyes, the heart's mirror; and the heart sees the object outside whatever it be, and sees many various objects, some green, others dark of hue, one crimson, the other blue; and it blames the one and praises the other, holds the one cheap and the other precious; but many an object shows him a fair face in the mirror when he looks at it, which will betray him if he be not on his guard. My mirror has much deceived me; for in it MY heart has seen a ray by which I am struck, which has taken shelter in me; and because of this my heart has failed me. I am ill-treated by my friend who deserts me for my enemy. Well can I accuse my mirror of treachery; for it has sinned exceedingly against me. I thought I had three friends: my heart and my two eyes together; but methinks they hate me. Where shall I find any more a friend, since these three are enemies who belong to me yet kill me? My servants presume overmuch who do all their own will and have no care of mine. Now, know I well of a truth from the action of those who have injured me: that a good master's love decays through keeping bad servants. He who associates with a bad servant cannot fail to lament it sooner or later, whatever come of it.

"Now will I speak to you again of the arrow which is given in trust to me and tell you how it is made and cut; but I fear much that I may fail in the matter; for the carved work of it is so magnificent that twill be no marvel if I fail. And yet I will apply all my diligence to say what I think of it. The notch and the feathers together are so close that if a man looks well at them there is but one dividing line like a narrow parting in the hair; but this line is so polished and straight, that without question there is nought in the notch which can be improved. The feathers are of such a hue as if they were gold or gilded; but gilding can add nothing; for the feathers, this know I well, were brighter still than gold. The feathers are the blonde tresses that I saw the other day at sea. This is the arrow that makes me love. God! What a priceless boon! If a man could have such a treasure, why should he desire any other wealth all his life? For my part, I could swear that I should desire nothing more; for merely the feathers and the notch would I not give away in exchange for Antioch. And since I prize these two things so much, who could duly appraise the value of the rest which is so fair and lovable, and so dear and so precious, that I am desirous and eager to behold myself mirrored again in the brow that God has made so bright that nor mirror nor emerald nor topaz would make any show beside it. But of all this, he who gazes at the brightness of the eyes has not a word to say; for to all those who behold them they seem two glowing candles. And who has so glib a tongue that he could describe the fashion of the well-shaped nose, and of the bright countenance where the rose overlays the lily so that it eclipses something of the lily in order the better to illuminate the face, and of the smiling little mouth which God made such on purpose that no one should see it and not think that it is laughing? And what of the teeth in her mouth? One is so close to the other that it seems that they all touch, and so that they might the better achieve this, Nature bestowed special pains, so that whoever should see them when the mouth opens would never dream that they were not of ivory or silver. So much there is to say and to recount in the describing of each thing—both of the chin and of the ears—that it would be no great marvel if I were to leave out something. Of the throat, I tell you, that in comparison with it, crystal is but dim. And the neck beneath her tresses is four times whiter than ivory. As much as is disclosed from the hem of the vest behind, to the clasp of the opening in front, saw I of the bare bosom uncovered, whiter, than is the new-fallen snow. My pain would indeed have been alleviated if I could have seen the whole of the arrow. Right willingly if I had known would I have said what the tip of the arrow is like: I did not see it; and it is not my own fault if I cannot tell the fashion of a thing that I have not seen. Love showed me then nought of it except the notch and the feathers; for the arrow was put in the quiver; the quiver is the tunic and the vest wherewith the maid was clad. Faith! This is the wound that kills me; this is the dart; this is the ray with which I am so cruelly inflamed. It is ignoble of me to be angry. Never for provocation or for war shall any pledge that I must seek of love be broken. Now let Love dispose of me as he ought to do with what is his; for I wish it, and this is my pleasure. Never do I seek that this malady should leave me; rather do I wish it to hold me thus for ever; and that from none may health come to me if health come not from that source whence the disease has come."

Great is the plaint of Alexander; but that which the damsel utters is not a whit less. All night she is in so great pain that she neither sleeps nor rests. Love has set in array within her a battle that rages and mightily agitates her heart; and which causes such anguish and torture that she weeps all night and complains and tosses and starts up, so that her heart all but stops beating. And when she has so grieved and sobbed and moaned and started and sighed, then she has looked in her heart to see who and of what worth was he for whose sake Love was torturing her. And when she has recalled each wandering thought, then she stretches herself and turns over; and turning, she turns to folly all the thinking she has done. Then she starts on another argument and says: "Fool! What does it matter to me if this youth is debonair and wise and courteous and valiant! All this is honour and advantage to him. And what care I for his beauty? Let his beauty depart with him—and so it will, for all I can do; never would I wish to take away aught of it. Take away? Nay, truly, that do I not assuredly. If he had the wisdom of Solomon, and if Nature had put so much beauty in him that she could not have put more in a human body, and if God had put in my hand the power to destroy all, I would not seek to anger him; but willingly if I could would I make him more wise and more beautiful. Faith! then, I do not hate him at all. And am I then on that account his lady? No, indeed, no more than I am another's. And wherefore do I think more of him if he does not please me more than another? I know not: I am all bewildered, for never did I think so much about any man living in the world. And if I had my wish I should see him always; never would I seek to take my eyes off him so much the sight of him delights me. Is this love? Methinks it is. Never should I have called on him so often if I had not loved him more than another. Yes, I love him: let that be granted. And shall I not have my desire? Yes, provided that I find favour in his eyes. This desire is wrong; but Love has taken such hold of me that I am foolish and dazed and to defend myself avails me nought herein; thus I must suffer Love's attack. I have indeed guarded myself thus wisely and for long against Love; never once before did I wish to do aught for him, but now I am too gracious to him. And what thanks does he owe me, since he cannot have service or kindness of me by fair means? It is by force that Love has tamed my pride; and I must needs be subject to his will. Now I wish to love; now I am under his tuition; now will Love teach me. And what? How I ought to serve him. Of that am I right well apprised. I am full wise in his service, for no one could find fault with me in this matter. No need is there henceforth for me to learn more. Love would have me, and

I would fain be wise without pride, gracious and courteous towards all, but the true love of one only. Shall I love them all for the sake of one? A fair mien should I show to each; but Love does not bid me to be a true love to every man. Love teaches nought but good. It is not for nothing that I have this name, and that I am called Soredamors. I ought to love, and I ought to be loved, and I wish to prove it by my name, if I can find fitting arguments. It is not without meaning that the first part of my name is the colour of gold; for the most beautiful are the blondest. Therefore I hold my name the fairer because it begins with the colour with which accords the finest gold. And the end recalls Love; for he who calls me by my right name ever calls Love to my mind. And the one half gilds the other with bright and yellow gilding; for Soredamors means the same thing as 'gilded with love'. Much, then, has Love honoured me, since he has gilded me with himself. Gilding of gold is not so fine as that which illumines me. And I shall set my care on this, that I may be of his gilding; nevermore will I complain of him. Now I love and shall always love. Whom? Truly, a fine question! Him whom Love bids me love; for no other shall ever have my love. What does it matter as he will never know it unless I tell him myself? What shall I do if I do not pray him for his love? For he who desires a thing ought indeed to request and pray for it. How? Shall I then pray him? Nay, indeed. Why not? It never happened that a woman did aught so witless as to beg a man for love unless she were more than common mad. I should be convicted of folly if I said with my mouth aught that might turn to my reproach. If he should know it from my mouth, I deem that he would hold me the cheaper for it, and would often reproach me with having been the first to pray for love. Never be Love so abased that I should go and entreat this man, since he would be bound to hold me the cheaper for it. Ah God! how will he ever know it, since I shall not tell him? As yet I have scarce suffered aught for which I need so distress myself. I shall wait till he perceives it, if he is ever destined to perceive it. He will know it well of a truth, I think, if ever he had aught to do with Love or heard tell of it by word of mouth. Heard tell! Now have I said foolish words. Love's lore is not so easy that a man becomes wise by speaking of it unless good experience be there too. Of myself I know this well; for never could I learn aught of it by fair speaking or by word of mouth; and yet I have been much at Love's school, and have often been flattered; but always have I kept aloof from him, and now he makes me pay dear for it; for now I know more of it than an ox does of ploughing. But of this I despair—that he never loved, perhaps, and if he does not love, and has not loved; then have I been sowing in the sea where no seed can take root; and there is nothing for it but to wait for him and to suffer till I see whether I can bring him into the right way by hints and covert words. I will so act that he will be certain of having my love if he dares to seek it. Thus the end of the whole matter is that I love him and am his. If he does not love me, I shall love him all the same."

Thus both he and she complain, and the one hides the case from the other; they have sorrow in the night and worse by day. In such pain they have, it seems to me, been a long while in Brittany until it came to the end of summer. Right at the beginning of October came messengers from the parts about Dover from London and from Canterbury to bring the king tidings that have troubled his heart. The messengers have told him this—that he may well tarry too long in Brittany; for he to whom he had entrusted his land, and had consigned so great a host of his subjects and of his friends, will now set himself in battle array against the king; and he has marched into London in order to hold the city against the hour that Arthur should have returned.

When the king heard the news he calls all his barons; for he was indignant and full of displeasure. That he may the better stir them up to confound the traitor, he says that all the blame for his toil and for his war is theirs; for through their persuasion he gave his land and put it into the hand of the traitor who is worse than Ganelon. There is not one who does not quite allow that the king has right and reason; for they all counselled him to do so; but the traitor will be ruined for it. And let him know well of a truth that in no castle or city will he be able so to protect his body that they do not drag him out of it by force. Thus they all assure the king and solemnly affirm and swear that they will give up the traitor or no longer hold their lands. And the king has it proclaimed through all Brittany that none who can bear arms in the host remain in the country without coming after him quickly.

All Brittany is moved: never was such a host seen as King Arthur assembled. When the ships moved out it seemed that everybody in the world was on the sea; for not even the waves were seen, so covered were they with ships. This fact is certain, that it seems from the stir that all Brittany is taking ship. Now have the ships made the passage; and the folk who have thronged together go into quarters along the shore. It came into Alexander's heart to go and beg the king to make him a knight; for if ever he is to win renown he will win it in this war. He takes his comrades with him, as his will urges him on to do what he has purposed. They have gone to the king's tent: the king was sitting before his tent. When he sees the Greeks coming he has called them before him. "Sirs," quoth he, "hide not from me what need brought you here." Alexander spoke for all and has told him his desire: "I am come," quoth he, "to pray you as I am bound to pray, my lord, for my companions and for myself, that you make us knights." The king replies: "Right gladly; and not a moment's delay shall there be, since you have made me this request." Then the king bids there be borne harness for twelve knights: done is what the king commands. Each asks for his own harness; and each has his own in his possession, fair arms and a good steed: each one has taken his harness. All the twelve were of like value, arms and apparel and horse; but the harness for Alexander's body was worth as much—if any one had cared to value or to sell it—as the arms of all the other twelve together. Straightway by the sea they disrobed and washed and bathed; for they neither wished nor deigned that any other bath should be heated for them. They made the sea their bath and tub.

The queen, who does not hate Alexander—rather does she love and praise and prize him much—hears of the matter. She wills to do him a great service; it is far greater than she thinks. She searches and empties all her chests till she has drawn forth a shirt of white silk very well wrought very delicate and very fine. There was no thread in the seams that was not of gold, or at the least of silver. Soredamors from time to time had set her hands to the sewing, and had in places sewn in beside the gold a hair from her head, both on the two sleeves and on the collar to see and to put to the test whether she could ever find a man who could distinguish the one from the other, however carefully he looked at it; for the hair was as shining and as golden as the gold or even more so. The queen takes the shirt and has given it to Alexander. Ah God! how great joy would Alexander have had if he had known what the queen is sending him. Very great joy would she too have had, who had sewn her hair there if she had known that her love was to have and wear it. Much comfort would she have had thereof; for she would not have loved all the rest of her hair so much as that which Alexander had. But neither he nor she knew it: great pity is it that they do not know. To the harbour where the youths are washing came the messenger of the queen; he finds the youths on the beach and has given the shirt to him, who is much delighted with it and who held it all the dearer for that it came from the queen. But if he had known the whole case he would have loved it still more; for he would not have taken all the world in exchange, but rather he would have treated it as a relic, I think, and would have worshipped it day and night.

Alexander delays no longer to apparel himself straightway. When he was clad and equipped he has returned to the tent of the king; and all his comrades together with him. The queen, as I think, had come to sit in the tent because she wished to see the new knights arrive. Well might one esteem them fair; but fairest of all was Alexander with the agile body. They are now knights; for the present I say no more about them. Henceforth shall I speak of the king and of the host which came to London. The greater part of the folk held to his side; but there is a great multitude of them against him. Count Engres musters his troops, all that he can win over to him by promise or by gift. When he had got his men together he has secretly fled by night; for he was hated by several and feared to be betrayed; but before he fled he took from London as much as he could of victuals of gold and of silver, and distributed it all to his folk. The tidings is told to the king—that the traitor is fled, and all his army with him, and that he had taken so much of victuals and goods from the city that the burgesses are impoverished and destitute and at a loss. And the king has replied just this: that never will he take ransom of the traitor, but will hang him if he can find or take him. Now all the host bestirs itself so much that they reached Windsor. At that day, however it be now, if any one wished to defend the castle, it would not have been easy to take; for the traitor enclosed it as soon as he planned the treason with treble walls and moats, and had strengthened the walls behind with sharpened stakes, so that they should not be thrown down by any siege-engine. He had spent great sums in strengthening it all June and July and August, in making walls, and bastions, and moats, and drawbridges, trenches, and breast-works, and barriers, and many a portcullis of iron, and a great tower of stones, hewn foursquare. Never had he shut the gate there for fear of attack. The castle stands on a high hill and below it runs Thames. The host is encamped on the river bank; on that day they had time for nought save encamping and pitching their tents.

The host has encamped on Thames: all the meadow is covered with tents, green and vermilion. The sun strikes on the colours and the river reflects their sheen for more than a full league. The defenders of the castle had come to take their pleasure along the strand with their lances only in their hands, their shields locked close in front of them, for they bore no arms but these. To their foes without they made it appear that they feared them not at all inasmuch as they had come unarmed. Alexander, on the other side, perceived the knights who go before them, playing a knightly game on horseback. Hot is his desire to meet with them; and he calls his comrades one after the other by their names: first Cornix, whom he greatly loved, then the stout Licorides, then Nabunal of Mycenae, and Acoriondes of Athens, and Ferolin of Salonica, and Calcedor from towards Africa, Parmenides and Francagel, Torin the Strong, and Pinabel, Nerius, and Neriolis. "Lords," quoth he, "a longing has seized me to go and make with lance and with shield acquaintance with those who come to tourney before us. I see full well that they take us for laggards and esteem us lightly—so it seems to me—since they have come here all unarmed to tourney before our faces. We have been newly dubbed knights; we have not yet shown our mettle to knights or at quintain. Too long have we kept our new lances virgin. Why were our shields made? Not yet have they been pierced or broken.

Such a gift avails us nought save for tour or for assault. Let us pass the ford, and let us attack them." All say: "We will not fail you." Each one says: "So may God save me, as I am not the man to fail you here." Now they gird on their swords, saddle and girth their steeds, mount and take their shields. When they had hung the shields from their necks, and taken the lances blazoned in quarterings; they all at once rush on to the ford; and the enemy lower their lances and ride quickly to strike them. But Alexander and his comrades knew well how to pay them back; and they neither spare them nor shirk nor yield a foot before them; rather each strikes his own foe so doughtily that there is no knight so good but he must void his saddle-bow. The Greeks did not take them for boys for cowards or for men bewildered. They have not wasted their first blows; for they have unhorsed thirteen. The noise of their blows and strokes has reached as far as to the army. In a short time the melee would have been desperate, if the enemy had dared to stand before them. The king's men run through the host to take their weapons, and dash into the water noisily, and the enemy turn to flight; for they see that it is not good to stay there. And the Greeks follow them, striking with lances and swords. Many heads there were cut open; but of the Greeks there was not a single one wounded. They have proved themselves well that day. But Alexander won the greatest distinction; for he leads away four knights bound to his person and taken prisoners. And the dead lie on the strand; for many there lay headless, and many wounded and maimed.

Alexander from courtesy gives and presents the first fruits of his knighthood to the queen. He does not wish that the king should have possession of the captives; for he would have had them all hanged. The queen has had them taken and has had them guarded in prison as accused of treason. Men speak of the Greeks throughout the army; all say that Alexander is right courteous and debonair as regards the knights whom he had taken inasmuch as he had not given them up to the king, who would have had them burned or hanged. But the king is in earnest in the matter. Forthwith he bids the queen that she come and speak to him and keep not her traitors; for it will behove her to give them up or he will take them against her will. Then the queen has come to the king; they have had converse together about the traitors as it behoved them; and all the Greeks had been left in the queen's tent with the ladies. Much do the twelve say to them, but Alexander does not say a word. Soredamors observed it; she had sat down near him. He has rested his cheek on his hand, and it seems that he is deep in thought. Thus have they sat full long till Soredamors saw on his arm and at his neck the hair with which she had made the seam. She has drawn a little nearer him, for now she has opportunity of speaking with him; but she considers beforehand how she can be the one to speak, and what the first word shall be; whether she will call him by his name; and she takes counsel of it with herself. "What shall I say first?" thinks she. "Shall I address him by his name, or as 'friend'. Friend? Not I. How then? Call him by his name? God! The word friend is so fair and so sweet to say. What if I dared to call him friend? Dared? What forbids it me? The fact that I think I should be telling a lie. A lie? I know not what it will be; but if I lie it will be a weight on my mind. For that reason it must be allowed that I should not desire to lie in the matter. God! He would not lie now a whit if he called me his sweet friend. And should I lie in so calling him? Both of us ought indeed to speak truth; but if I lie the wrong will be his. And why is his name so hard to me that I wish to add a name of courtesy? It seems to me there are too many letters in it, and I should become tongue-tied in the middle. But if I called him friend, I should very quickly say this name. But just because I fear to stumble in the other name, I would have given of my heart's-blood if only his name might have been 'my sweet friend'."

She delays so long in thus thinking that the queen returns from the king, who had sent for her. Alexander sees her coming, and goes to meet her, and asks her what the king commands to be done with his prisoners, and what will be their fate. "Friend," says she, "he requires me to yield them up to his discretion and to let him do his justice on them. He is very wroth that I have not yet given them up to him and I must send them; for I see no other way out." Thus they have passed this day; and on the morrow the good and loyal knights have assembled together before the royal tent to pronounce justice and judgment as to with what penalty and with what torture the four traitors should die. Some doom that they be flayed, others that they be hanged or burnt, and the king himself deems that traitors should be drawn. Then he bids them be brought: they are brought; he has them bound, and tells them that they shall not be quartered till they are in view of the castle, so that those within shall see them. When the parley is done, the king addresses Alexander and calls him his dear friend. "Friend," quoth he, "I saw you yesterday make a fair attack and a fair defence. I will give you the due guerdon: I increase your following by 500 Welsh knights and by 1000 footmen of this land. When I shall have finished my war, in addition to what I have given you, I will have you crowned king of the best realm in Wales. Market-towns and strong castles, cities and halls, will I give you, meanwhile, till the land shall be given to you which your father holds and of which you must become emperor." Alexander heartily thanks the king for this grant; and his comrades thank him likewise. All the barons of the Court say that the honour which the king designs for him is well vested in Alexander.

When Alexander sees his men his comrades and his footmen, such as the king willed to give him, then they begin to sound horns and trumpets throughout the host. Good and bad all, I would have you know, without exception take their arms, those of Wales and of Brittany of Scotland and of Cornwall; for from all sides without fail strong reinforcements had come in for the host. Thames had shrunk; for there had been no rain all the summer; rather there had been such a drought that the fish in it were dead and the ships leaky in the harbour; and one could pass by the ford there where the water was widest of a hair and has delight and joyaunce thereof; but the host has crossed Thames; some beset the valley and others mount the height. The defenders of the castle perceive it, and see coming the wondrous host which is preparing outside to overthrow and take the castle; and they prepare to defend it. But before any attack is made the king has the traitors dragged by four horses round the castle, through the valleys, and over mounds and hillocks. Count Engres is sore grieved when he sees those whom he held dear dragged round his castle; and the others were much dismayed; but for all the dismay that they feel thereat they have no desire to surrender. Needs must they defend themselves; for the king displays openly to all his displeasure and his wrath; and full well they see that if he held them he would make them die shamefully.

When the four had been drawn and their limbs lay o'er the field, then the attack begins; but all their toil is vain; for howsoever they may hurl and throw their missiles, they can avail nought. And yet they try hard; they throw and hurl a thick cloud of bolts and javelins and darts. The catapults and slings make a great din on all sides; arrows and round stone fly likewise in confusion as thick as rain mingled with hail. Thus they toil all day: these defend, and those attack until night separates them, one from the other, nor need they trouble to flee, nor do they see. And the king on his part has it cried through the host and made known what gift that man will have of him by whom the castle shall have been taken: a goblet of very great price, worth fifteen golden marks, the richest in his treasure, will he give him. The goblet will be very fair and rich; and he whose judgement goes not astray ought to hold it dearer for the workmanship than for the material. The goblet is very precious in workmanship, and if I were to disclose the whole truth, the jewels on the outside were worth more than the workmanship or the gold. If he by whom the castle will be taken is but a foot soldier, he shall have the cup. And if it is taken by a knight, never shall he seek any reward besides the cup; but he will have it if it can be found in the world. When this matter was proclaimed Alexander, who went each evening to see the queen, had not forgotten his custom. On this evening he had again gone thither; they were seated side by side, both Alexander and the queen. Before them Soredamors was sitting alone nearest to them; and she looked at him as gladly as though she would not have preferred to be in Paradise. The queen held Alexander by his right hand, and looked at the golden thread which had become greatly tarnished; and the hair was becoming yet fairer whereas the gold thread was growing pale; and she remembered by chance that Soredamors had done the stitching and she laughed thereat. Alexander observed it and asks her, if it may be told, to tell him what makes her laugh. The queen delays to tell him, and looks towards Soredamors, and has called her before her. She has come very gladly and kneels before her. Alexander was much joyed when he saw her approach so near that he could have touched her; but he has not so much courage as to dare even to look at her; but all his senses have so left him that he has almost become dumb. And she, on the other hand, is so bewildered that she has no use of her eyes, but fixes her gaze on the ground, and dares not direct it elsewhere. The queen greatly marvels; she sees her now pale, now flushed, and notes well in her heart the bearing and appearance of each and of the two together. She sees clearly and truly, it seems to her, judging by the changes of colour, that these are signs of love; but she does not wish to cause them anguish: she feigns to know nothing of what she sees. She did just what it behoved her to do; for she gave no look or hint save that she said to the maiden: "Damsel, look yonder and tell—hide it not from us—where the shirt that this knight has donned was sewn, and whether you had a hand in it, and put in it somewhat of yours?" The maiden is ashamed to say it; nevertheless, she tells it to him gladly; for she wishes that he should hear the truth; and he has such joy of hearing it when she tells and describes to him the making of the shirt, that with great difficulty he restrains himself when he sees the hair from worshipping and doing reverence to it. His comrades and the queen, who were there with him, cause him great distress and annoyance; for on account of them he refrains from raising it to his eyes and to his lips where he would fain have pressed it if he had not thought that they would see him. He is blithe that he has so much of his lady-love; but he does not think or expect to have ever any other boon of her. His desire makes him fear; nevertheless, when he is alone he kisses it more than a hundred thousand times when he has left the queen. Now it seems to him that he was born in a lucky hour. Very great joy does he have of it all night, but he takes good care that no one sees him. When he has lain down in his bed, he delights and consoles him self fruitlessly with that in which there is no delight; all night he embraces the shirt, and when he beholds the hair he thinks he is lord of all the world. Truly Love makes a wise man a fool: since he has joy, he will change his pastime before the bright dawn and the sunlight. The traitors are holding counsel as to what they will be able to do and what will become of them. Long time they will be able to defend the castle; that is a certainty if they apply themselves to the defence; but they know that the king is of so fierce a courage that in all his life he will never turn away until he has taken it; then they must needs die. And if they surrender the castle they expect no grace for that. Thus the one lot or the other; it has fallen out ill for them; for they have no reinforcement, and they see death on all sides. But the end of their deliberation is that to-morrow, before day appears, they resolve to issue forth secretly from the castle, and to fall on the host unarmed, and the knights asleep, since they will still be lying in their beds. Before these have awakened, apparelled and equipped, themselves, they will have made such slaughter that ever hereafter shall be related the battle of that night. To this plan all the traitors cling from desperation, for they have no confidence as to their lives. Lack of hope as to the outcome emboldens them to the battle, for they see no issue for themselves except through death or prison. Such an issue is no wholesome one, nor need they trouble to flee, nor do they see where they could find refuge if they should have fled; for the sea and their enemies are around them, and they in the midst. No longer do they tarry at their council: now they apparel and arm themselves, and issue forth towards the north-west by an ancient postern towards that side whence they thought that those of the host would least expect to see them come. In serried ranks they sallied forth: of their men they made five battalions; and there were no less than two thousand foot-soldiers well equipped for battle and a thousand knights in each. This night neither star nor moon had shown its rays in the sky; but before they had reached the tents the moon began to rise, and, I believe that just to vex them, it rose earlier than it was wont; and God who wished to injure them lit up the dark night, for He had no care of their army; rather He hated them for their sin with which they were tainted for traitors and treason which God hates more than any other crime; so the moon began to shine because it was doomed to injure them.

The moon was veritably hostile to them; for it shone on their glittering shields; and the helmets likewise greatly embarrass them, for they reflect the light of the moon for the sentries who were set to guard the host see them; and they cry throughout all the host: "Up, knights! Up, rise quickly! Take your arms, arm yourselves! Behold the traitors upon us!" Through all the host they spring to arms; they rouse themselves and don with haste their harness, as men must do in case of stress. Never did a single one of them stir forth till they were fully equipped; and all mounted on their steeds. While they are arming, the enemy, on the other hand, who greatly desire the battle, are bestirring themselves, so that they may take them unawares and likewise find them unarmed; and they send forth their men whom they had divided into five bands. Some kept beside the wood; others came along the river; the third placed themselves in the plain; and the fourth were in a valley; and the fifth battalion spurs along the moat that surrounded a rock, for they thought to swoop down impetuously among the tents. But they have not found a road that they could follow, or a way that was not barred; for the king's men block their way as they very proudly defy them and reproach them with treason. They engage with the iron heads of their lances, so that they splinter and break them; they come to close quarters with swords; and champion strikes champion to the ground and makes him bite the dust; each side strikes down its foes, and as fiercely as lions devouring whatsoever they can seize rush on their prey; so fiercely do they rush on their foe—aye, and more fiercely. On both sides, of a truth, there was very great loss of life at that first attack; but reinforcements come for the traitors, who defend themselves very fiercely, and sell their lives dear when they can keep them no longer. On four sides they see their battalions coming to succour them; and the king's men gallop upon them as fast as they can spur. They rush to deal them such blows on the shields, that together with the wounded they have overthrown more than five hundred of them. The Greeks spare them not at all. Alexander is not idle, for he exerts himself to act bravely. In the thickest of the fray he rushes so impetuously to smite a traitor, that neither shield nor hauberk availed one whit to save that traitor from being thrown to the ground. When Alexander has made a truce with him forsooth, he pays his attentions to another—attentions in which he does not waste or lose his pains. He serves him in such valiant sort that he rends his soul from his body; and the house remains without a tenant. After these two Alexander picks a quarrel with a third: he strikes a right noble court knight through both flanks in such wise that the blood gushes out of the wound on the opposite side; and the soul takes leave of the body, for the foe man has breathed it forth. Many a one he kills; many a one he maims; for like the forked lightning he attacks all those that he seeks out. Him whom he strikes with lance or sword, neither corselet nor shield protects. His comrades also are very lavish in spilling blood and brains; well do they know how to deal their blows. And the king's men cut down so many that they break and scatter them like common folk distraught. So many dead lie o'er the fields and so long has the scour lasted, that the battle-array was broken up a long while before it was day; and the line of dead down along the river extended five leagues. Count Engres leaves his standard in the battle and steals away; and he has taken seven of his companions together with him. He has returned towards his castle by so hidden a way that he thinks that no one sees; but Alexander marks him; for he sees them flee from the host, and thinks to steal away and meet them, so that no one will know where he has gone. But before he was in the valley he saw as many as thirty knights coming after him along a path, six of whom were Greeks, and the other four-and-twenty Welsh; for they thought that they would follow him at a distance until it should come to the pinch. When Alexander perceived them he stopped to wait, and marks which way those who are returning to the castle take until he sees them enter. Then he begins to meditate on a very hazardous venture and on a very wondrous stratagem. And when he had finished all his thinking, he turns towards his comrades, and thus has related and said to them: "Lords," quoth he, "without gainsaying me, if ye wish to have my love, whether it be prompted by folly or wisdom, grant me my wish." And they have granted it; for never will they refuse him anything that he may choose to do. "Let us change our insignia," quoth he; "let us take shields and lances from the traitors that we have slain. Thus we shall go towards the castle, and the traitors within will think that we are of their party, and whatever the requital may be the doors will be opened to us. Know ye in what wise we shall requite them? We shall take them all or dead or living if God grant it us; and if any of you repent you know that as long as I live, I shall never love him with a good heart."

All grant him his will: they go and seize the shields from the Dead; and they arrive with this equipment. And the folk of the castle had mounted to the battlements of the tower, for they recognised the shields full well and think that they belong to their own men; for they were unsuspicious of the ambush which lurks beneath the shields. The porter opens the door to them and has received them within. He is so beguiled and deceived that he does not address them at all; and not one of them breathes a word, but they pass on mute and silent, feigning such grief that they drag their lances behind them and bend beneath their shields, so that it seems that they are sorrowing greatly; and they go in whatever direction they wish until they have passed the three walls. Up yonder they find so many foot-soldiers and knights with the count, I cannot tell you the number of them; but they were all unarmed except the eight alone, who had returned from the army; and these even were preparing to take off their armour. But they might well prove over-hasty; for those who have come upon them up yonder no longer hid themselves, but put their steeds to the gallop. All press on their stirrups and fall upon them and attack them, so that they strike dead thirty-and-one before they have given the challenge. The traitors are much dismayed thereat and cry, "Betrayed! Betrayed!" But Alexander and his friends are not confused; for as soon as they find them all unarmed they test their swords well there. Even three of those whom they found armed have they so served that they have only left five. Count Engres has rushed forward, and before the eyes of all goes to strike Calcedor on his golden shield, so that he throws him to the ground dead. Alexander is much grieved when he sees his comrade slain; he well-nigh goes mad with the fury that comes upon him. His reason is dimmed with anger, but his strength and courage are doubled, and he goes to strike the count with such a mighty force that his lance breaks; for willingly, if he could, would he avenge the death of his friend. But the count was of great strength, a good and bold knight to boot, such that there would not have been a better in the world if he had not been disloyal and a traitor. The count, on his side, prepares to give him such a blow that he bends his lance, so that it altogether splinters and breaks; but the shield does not break and the one knight does not shake the other from his seat any more than he would have shaken a rock, for both were very strong. But the fact that the count was in the wrong mightily vexes and weakens him. The one grows furious against the other, and both have drawn their swords, since they had broken their lances. And there would have been no escape if these two champions had wished further to prolong the fight; one or the other would have had to die forthwith at the end. But the count does not dare to stand his ground, for he sees his men slain around him, who, being unarmed, were taken unawares. And the king's men pursue them fiercely, and hack and hew, and cleave, and brain them, and call the count a traitor. When he hears himself accused of treason, he flees for refuge towards his keep; and his men flee with him. And their enemies who fiercely rush after take them captive; they let not a single one escape of all those that they catch. They kill and slay so many that I do not think that more than seven reached a place of safety. When the traitors entered the keep, they are stayed at the entrance; for their pursuers had followed them so close that their men would have got in if the entrance had been open. The traitors defend themselves well; for they expect succour from them who were arming in the town below. But by the advice of Nabunal, a Greek who was very wise, the way was held against the reinforcements, so that they could not come in time, for they had tarried over-long from lukewarmness and indolence. Up there into that fortress there was only one single entry; if the Greeks stop up that entrance, they will have no need to fear the coming of any force from which ill may befall them. Nabunal bids and exhorts that twenty of them go to defend the outer gateway; for easily there might they press in that way to attack and overwhelm them—foemen who would do them harm if they had strength and power to do so. "Let a score of men go to defend the gateway, and let the other ten assail the keep from without, so that the count may not shut himself up inside." This is what Nabunal advises: the ten remain in the melee before the entrance of the keep; the score go to the gate. They have delayed almost too long; for they see coming a company, flushed and heated with desire of fighting, in which there were many crossbow-men and foot-soldiers of divers equipment, bearing diverse arms. Some carried light missiles, and others, Danish axes, Turkish lances and swords, arrows and darts and javelins. Very heavy would have been the reckoning that the Greeks would have had to pay, peradventure, if this company had come upon them, but they did not come in time. By the wisdom and by the prudence of Nabunal, they forestalled them and kept them without. When the reinforcements see that they are shut out, then they remain idle, for they see well that by attacking they will be able to accomplish nought in the matter. Then there rises a mourning and a cry of women and of little children, of old men and of youths, so great that if it had thundered from the sky those within the castle would not have heard aught of it. The Greeks greatly rejoice thereat; for now they all know of a surety that never by any chance will the count escape being taken. They bid four of them mount in haste to the battlements of the wall to see that those without do not from any quarter, by any stratagem or trick, press into the castle to attack them. The sixteen have returned to the ten who are fighting. Now was it bright daylight, and now the ten had forced their way into the keep, and the count, armed with an axe, had taken his stand beside a pillar where he defends himself right fiercely. He cleaves asunder all who come within his reach. And his followers range themselves near him; in their last day's work they take such good vengeance that they spare not their strength at all. Alexander's knights lament that there were no more than thirteen of them left though even now there were twenty-and-six. Alexander well-neigh raves with fury when he sees such havoc among his men who are thus killed and wounded, but he is not slow to revenge. He has found at hand, by his side, a long and heavy beam, and goes to strike therewith a traitor; and neither the foeman's shield nor hauberk availed him a whit against being borne to the ground. After him, he attacks the count; in order to strike well he raises the beam; and he deals him such a blow with his square-hewn beam that the axe falls from his hands; and he was so stunned and so weak, that if he had not leaned against the wall his feet would not have supported him.

With this blow the battle ceases. Alexander leaps towards the count and seizes him in such wise that he cannot move. No need is there to tell more of the others, for easily were they vanquished when they saw their lord taken. They capture them all with the count and lead them away in dire shame even as they had deserved. Of all this, King Arthur's host who were without, knew not a word; but in the morning when the battle was ended they had found their shields among the bodies; and the Greeks were raising a very loud lamentation for their lord but wrongly. On account of his shield which they recognise they one and all make great mourning, and swoon over his shield, and say that they have lived too long. Cornix and Nerius swoon; and when they come to themselves they blame their lives for being yet whole in them. And so do Torins and Acoriondes; the tears ran in streams from their eyes right on to their breasts. Life and joy are but vexation to them. And above all Parmenides has dishevelled and torn his hair. These five make so great a mourning for their lord that greater there cannot be. But they disquiet themselves in vain; instead of him, they are bearing away another; and yet they think that they are bearing away their lord. The other shields too cause them much sorrow by reason whereof they think that the bodies are those of their comrades; and they swoon and lament over them. But the shields lie one and all; for of their men there was but one slain who was named, Neriolis. Him truly would they have borne away had they known the truth. But they are in as great distress about the others as about him; and they have borne and taken them all. About all but one they are mistaken; but even like a man who dreams, who believes a lie instead of truth, the shields made them believe that this lie was true. They are deceived by the shields. They have set out with the bodies of the slain, and have come to their tents where there were many folk lamenting; but one and all of the others joined in the lament the Greeks were making. There was a great rally to their mourning. Now Soredamors, who hears the wailing and the lament for her friend, thinks and believes that she was born in an evil hour. For anguish and grief she loses memory and colour; and this it is that grieves and wounds her much, but she dare not openly show her grief; she has hidden her mourning in her heart. And yet, if any one had marked it, he would have seen by her countenance and by her outer semblance, that she suffered great pain and sorrow of body; but each one had enough to do to utter his own grief and recked nought of another's. Each was lamenting his own sorrow; for they find their kinsmen and their friends in evil case; for the river-bank was covered with them. Each lamented his own loss which is heavy and bitter. There the son weeps for the father, and here the father for the son; this man is swooning over his cousin, and this other, over his nephew; thus in each place they lament, fathers and brothers and kinsmen. But conspicuous above all is the lament that the Greeks were making although they might, with justice, expect great joy; for the greatest mourning of all the host will soon turn to joy.

The Greeks are raising great lamentation without; and those who are within are at great pains how to let them hear that whereof they will have much joy. They disarm and bind their prisoners who beg and pray them to take now their heads; but the king's men do not will or deign to do this. Rather, they say that they will keep them until they deliver them to the king, who then will give them their due, so that their merits will be requited. When they had disarmed them all they have made them mount the battlements in order to show them to their folk below. Much does this kindness displease them; since they saw their lord taken and bound they were not a whit glad. Alexander, from the wall above, swears by God and the saints of the world that never will he let a single one of them live, but will kill them all; and none shall stay his hand if they do not all go to yield themselves up to the king before he can take them. "Go," quoth he, "I bid you to my lord without fail, and place yourselves at his mercy. None of you save the count here has deserved death. Never shall ye lose limb or life if ye place yourselves at his mercy. If ye do not redeem yourselves from death merely by crying 'Mercy', very little confidence can ye have in your lives or in your bodies. Issue forth, all disarmed, to meet my lord, the king, and tell him from me, that Alexander sends you. Ye will not lose your pains; for the king, my lord, will remit for you all his wrath and indignation, so gentle and debonair is he. And if ye will do otherwise, ye will have to die; for never will pity for you seize him." All of them together believe this counsel; they do not stop till they reach the king's tent; and they have all fallen at his feet. Now is it known throughout the host what they have told and related. The king mounts, and all have mounted with him; and they come spurring to the castle, for no longer do they delay.

Alexander issues forth from the castle towards the king to whom his sight was well pleasing; and he has yielded up to him the count. And the king has no longer delayed to do justice on him immediately; but he greatly praises and extols Alexander; and all the rest greet him with ceremony and praise and extol him loudly. There is none who does not manifest joy. The mourning that they were formerly making yields to joy; but no joy can be compared with that of the Greeks. The king bids them give him the cup which was very magnificent and worth fifteen marks; and he tells and assures him that there is nought however dear, save the crown and the queen, that he will not yield to him if he will to ask it. Alexander dares not utter his desire in this matter, yet knows well that the king would not disappoint him if he asked for his lady-love; but he greatly fears that he might displease her, who would have had great joy thereat; for rather does he wish grief for himself without her than to have her without her will. Therefore he begs and requests a respite; for he does not wish to make his request till he know her pleasure in the matter; but he has sought neither respite nor delay in possessing himself of the golden cup. He takes the cup and generously entreats my Lord Gawain until he accepts this cup from him; but with exceeding great reluctance has that knight accepted it. When Soredamors has heard the true news about Alexander much did it please and delight her. When she knew that he is alive she has such joy thereof, that it seems to her never can she have grief for an hour; but too long it seems to her does he tarry to come as he is wont. Soon she will have what she desires; for the two vie with each other in their yearning for the same thing.

Alexander greatly longed to be able to feast his eyes on her if only with one sweet look. Already for a long time would he fain have come to the queen's tent if he had not been kept elsewhere. Delay displeased him much, so soon as ever he could he came to the queen in her tent. The queen has met him; for she knew much of his thought without his ever having spoken; but well had she perceived it. As he enters the tent she salutes him and takes pains to greet him with due ceremony; well she knows what occasion brings him. Because she wishes to serve him to his liking she puts Soredamors by his side; and they three were alone conversing far from the others. The queen is the first to begin; for she had no doubt at all that they loved each other, he her, and she him. Well she thinks to know it for a certainty and is convinced that Soredamors could not have a better lover. She was seated between them and begins a discourse which came aptly and in season.

"Alexander," quoth the queen, "Love is worse than hatred, for it grieves and bewilders its devotee. Lovers know not what they do when the one hides his feelings from the other. In Love there is much grievous toil: he who does not make a bold beginning in the laying of the foundation can scarce put on the coping-stone. The saying goes that there is nothing so difficult to cross as the threshold. I wish to instruct you about Love; for well I know that Love is using you badly. For this reason have I taken you to task; and take care that you conceal nought of it from me, for clearly have I seen from the countenances of each, that of two hearts you have made one. Never seek to hide it from me. You act very foolishly in that the twain of you tell not your thoughts; for you are killing each other by this concealment; you will be Love's murderers. Now, I counsel you that you seek not to satisfy your love by rape or by lust. Unite yourselves in honourable marriage. Thus as it seems to me your love will last long. I venture to assure you of this, that if you have a mind for it I will bring about the marriage."

When the queen had disburdened her heart Alexander on his side disclosed his. "Lady," quoth he, "I deny nought whereof you charge me; rather do I quite admit all that you say. Never do I seek to be free from Love, so as not always to devote myself to it. This that you of your pity have told me greatly pleases and delights me. Since you know my will, I know not why I should any longer conceal it from you. Very long ago if I had dared I would have confessed it; for the concealment has pained me much. But perhaps this maiden would in no wise will that I should be hers, and she mine. If she grants me nought of herself, yet still I give myself to her." At these words she trembled; and she does not refuse this gift. She betrays the wish of her heart both in words and looks; for trembling she gives herself to him, and says that never will she make any reservation of will or heart or person; but will be wholly at the queen's command and will do all her pleasure. The queen embraces them both and gives the one to the other. Laughing, she says: "I yield to thee, Alexander, the body of thy love. Well I know that thou art not alarmed thereat. Let who will look askance thereat; I give you the one to the other. Hold, thou, what is thine, and thou, Alexander, what is thine." She has what is hers, and he, what is his; he, all of her, and she, all of him. The betrothal took place that very day at Windsor, without a doubt with the consent and permission of my Lord Gawain and the king. None could tell, I ween, of the magnificence and feasting, of the joy and pleasure so great that at the wedding there would not have been more. But inasmuch as it would displease most people, I will not waste or spend one word thereon, for I wish to apply myself to the telling of something better.

On one day at Windsor had Alexander so much honour and joy as pleased him. Three joys and three honours he had: One was for the castle that he took; the second, for that which King Arthur promised that he would give him when the war was ended—the best realm in Wales—that day Arthur made him king in his halls. The greatest joy was the third because his lady-love was queen of the chessboard whereof he was king. Before five months were passed Soredamors was great with human seed and grain; and she bore it till her time. Such was the seed in its germ that the fruit came according to its kind. A fairer child there could not be, before or after. They called the child Cliges.

Born was Cliges, in memory of whom this story was put into French. Ye shall hear me tell fully and relate of him and of his knightly service, when he shall have come to such an age, that he will be destined to grow in fame. But meanwhile it happened in Greece that the emperor who ruled Constantinople came to his end. He was dead; he needs must die, for he could not pass the term appointed. But before his death he assembled all the high barons of his land in order to send and fetch Alexander, his son, who was in Britain where right willingly he tarried. The messengers depart from Greece; o'er the sea they take their voyage; and there a tempest overtakes them which sorely distresses their ship and their folk. They were all drowned in the sea save one treacherous fellow, a renegade, who loved Alis, the younger son, more than Alexander, the elder. When he had escaped from the sea he has returned to Greece; and related that they had all been drowned in a storm on the sea when they were returning from Britain; and were bringing away their lord; not one of them had escaped save he, only, from the storm and the peril. His lying tale was believed. Unopposed and unchallenged they take Alis and crown him: they give to him the empire of Greece. But it was not long ere Alexander knew for a certainty that Alis was emperor. Forthwith he has taken leave of King Arthur; for by no means will he resign his land to his brother without a fight. The king in no wise deters him from the plan; rather he bids him lead away with him so great a multitude of Welsh Scots and Cornishmen, that his brother will not dare to stand his ground when he shall see the host assembled. Alexander might have led away a great force had he willed. But he has no care to destroy his people if his brother will answer him in such wise as to perform his promise. He led away forty knights and Soredamors and his son. These two would he not leave behind; for they were meet to be greatly loved. They sailed from Shoreham where they took leave of the whole court; they had fair winds; the ship ran much more swiftly than a fleeing stag. Before the month had passed, I ween, they came to anchor before Athens, a city very magnificent and strong. The emperor, in sooth, was staying in the city; and there was a great gathering there of the high barons of the land. As soon as they were arrived Alexander sends a trusted servant into the city to know if he could have a fitting welcome there or if they will deny that he is their rightful lord.

The bearer of this message was a courteous and prudent knight whom men called Acorionde, a man of wealth and eloquence; and he was much esteemed in the land, for he was a native of Athens.

From of old his forbears had always had very high lordship in the city. When he had heard told that the emperor was in the city he goes to contend with him for the crown on behalf of Alexander, his brother; and he cannot pardon him for that he has kept it unjustly. Straight into the palace has he come; and finds many a one who greets him fair; but he gives no answer nor does he say a word to any man who greets him; rather he waits until he may hear what will and what mind they have toward their true lord. He does not stop till he reaches the emperor; he greets him not, nor bows to him, nor calls him emperor. "Alis," quoth he, "I bear thee a message from Alexander who is out yonder in this harbour. Hear what word thy brother sends to thee: He asks of thee what is his and seeks nought that is contrary to justice. Constantinople which thou holdest ought to be his; and will be his. Neither reasonable nor right would it be that there should be discord 'twixt you twain. Take my counsel, and come to terms with him, and give him the Crown in peace; for it is right meet that thou yield it to him."

Alis replies: "Fair sweet friend, thou hast taken on thyself a foolish errand in that thou hast brought this message. No comfort hast thou brought to me, for I know well that my brother is dead. It would be a great consolation to me if he were alive and I knew it. Never will I believe it till I see him. He is dead a while ago; and that is a grief to me. Not a word that thou sayest do I believe. And if he is alive wherefore comes he not? Never need he fear that I will not give him land in plenty. He is mad if he keeps aloof from me; and if he serve me he will never be the worse for it. Never

will there be any man that will hold the crown and the empire against me."
Acorionde hears that the emperor's reply is not favourable; but by no fear is
he withheld from speaking his mind. "Alis," quoth he, "may God confound
me if the matter is left thus. On thy brother's behalf I defy thee, and on his
behalf, as is meet, I exhort all those that I see here to leave thee and come
over to his side. It is meet that they cleave to him; him ought they to make
their lord. He who is loyal, let now his loyalty appear."

With this word he leaves the court; and the emperor, on his side,
summons those in whom he most trusts. From them he seeks counsel as
to his brother who thus challenges him, and seeks to know if he can fully
trust them not to give support or aid to him in this attack. Thus he hopes to
prove each one; but he finds not even one to cleave to him with regard to the
war; rather do they bid him remember the war that Eteocles waged against
Polynices, who was his own brother, in which the one killed the other with
his own hands. "A like thing may chance with regard to you if you are bent
on pursuing war; and the land will be ruined by reason thereof." Therefore
they counsel him to seek such a peace as may be reasonable and honourable;
and that the one make no unreasonable demands on the other. Now Alis
hears that if he does not make a fair covenant with his brother, all the barons
will desert him; and he said they will never desire an arrangement which he
cannot equitably make; but he establishes in the covenant that whate'er the
outcome of the matter the crown remain to him.

In order to make firm and lasting peace Alis sends one of his masters-
at-arms and bids Alexander come to him and rule all the land; but that he
do Alis so much honour as to allow him to keep the name of emperor and
let him have the crown; thus, if he will, can this covenant be made 'twixt
the twain of them. When this thing was related and told to Alexander, his
folk have mounted with him and have come to Athens. With joy were they
received; but it does not please Alexander that his brother should have the
lordship of the empire and of the crown if he give him not his promise
that never will he wed woman; but that after him, Cliges shall be emperor
of Constantinople. Thus are the brothers reconciled. Alexander makes him
swear; and Alis grants and warrants him that never as long as he shall
live will he take wife. They are reconciled and remain friends. The barons
manifest great joy; they take Alis for emperor; but before Alexander come
affairs great and small. Whatever he commands and says is done; and little
is done except through him. Alis has no longer anything but the name—
for he is called emperor—but Alexander is served and loved; and he who
does not serve him through love, must needs do so through fear. By means
of love and fear he rules all the land according to his will. But he whose
name is Death spares no man, weak or strong, but slays and kills them all.

Alexander was destined to die; for a sickness for which there was no remedy took him in its grip; but before death came upon him he sent for his son and said: "Fair son, Cliges, never canst thou know how much prowess and valour thou shalt have if thou go not first to prove thyself at King Arthur's court on both the Britons and the French. If fate lead thee thither, so bear and demean thyself that thou remain unknown till thou hast proved thyself on the flower of the knighthood at the court. I counsel thee that thou believe me in this matter; and that if opportunity comes thou fear not to put thy fortune to the test with thy uncle, my Lord Gawain. Prithee forget not this."

After this exhortation he lived not long. Soredamors had such grief thereat that she could not live after him. For sheer grief she died when he died. Alis and Cliges both mourned for them as they were bound; but in time they ceased to mourn. For all mourning must come to an end; all things needs must cease. Ill is it to prolong mourning, for no good can come of it. The mourning has ceased; and for a long time after the emperor has refrained from taking wife, for he would fain strive after loyalty. But there is no court in all the world that is pure from evil counsel. Nobles often leave the right way through the evil counsels to which they give credence, so that they do not keep loyalty. Often do his men come to the emperor, and they give him counsel, and exhort him to take a wife. So much do they exhort and urge him, and each day do they so much beset him, that through their great importunity, they have turned him from his loyalty, and he promises to do their will. But he says that she who is to be lady of Constantinople must needs be very graceful and fair and wise, rich and of high degree. Then his counsellors say to him that they will make ready and will hie them into the German land to sue for the daughter of the emperor. They counsel him to take her; for the emperor of Germany is very mighty and very powerful and his daughter is so fair that never in Christendom was there a damsel of such beauty. The emperor grants them all their suit; and they set out on the way like folk well equipped. They have ridden in their days' journeys until they found the emperor at Ratisbon, and asked him to give his elder daughter for their lord's behalf.

The emperor was full blithe at this embassy and gladly has he promised them his daughter; for he in no wise abases himself by so doing and abates not one jot of his dignity. But he says that he had promised to give her to the Duke of Saxony; and that the Greeks could not take her away unless the emperor came and brought a mighty force, so that the duke could not do him hurt or injury on the way back to Greece.

When the messengers had heard the emperor's reply they take their leave and set out once more for home. They have returned to their lord and have told him the reply. And the emperor has taken chosen men, knights proven in arms, the best that he has found, and he takes with him his nephew, for whose sake he had vowed that he would never take wife as long as he lived. But in no wise will he keep this vow if he can win to reach Cologne. On a day appointed he departs from Greece and shapes his course towards Germany; for he will not fail for blame nor for reproach to take a wife. But his honour will wane thereby. He does not stop till he reaches Cologne where the emperor had established his court for a festival held for all Germany. When the company of the Greeks had come to Cologne there were so many Greeks and so many Germans from the north, that more than sixty thousand had to find quarters outside the town.

Great was the gathering of folk, and very great was the joy that the two emperors showed, for they were right glad to meet face to face. In the palace which was very long was the assembly of the barons; and now the emperor sent for his beautiful daughter. The maiden did not tarry. Straightway she came into the palace; and she was fair, and so well shaped, just as God Himself had made her; for it pleased Him greatly to show such workmanship as to make people marvel. Never did God who fashioned her give to man a word that could express so much beauty, that there was not in her still more beauty.

Fenice was the maiden named, and not without reason; for just as the bird Phoenix is fairest above all others and there cannot be more than one phoenix at a time, so Fenice, I deem, had no peer for beauty. It was a wonder and a marvel, for never again could Nature attain to framing her like. Inasmuch as I should say less than the truth, I will not in words describe arms nor body nor head nor hands; for if I had a thousand years to live and each day had doubled my wisdom I should still waste all my time, and yet never express the truth of it. I know well that if I meddled with it I should exhaust all my wisdom upon it and should squander all my pains; for it would be wasted pains. The maiden has hastened and has come into the palace with head uncovered and face bare; and the sheen of her beauty sheds greater light in the palace than four carbuncles would have done. Now Cliges had doffed his cloak in presence of his uncle, the emperor. The day was somewhat cloudy but so beauteous were the twain, both the maid and he, that there shot forth from their beauty a ray with which the palace glowed again, just as the sun shines bright and ruddy in the morning.

To describe the beauty of Cliges I will limn you a portrait, the traits of which shall be very briefly told. He was in the flower of his youth, for he was about fifteen years old. He was fairer and more comely than Narcissus' who saw his own reflection in the fountain beneath the elm, and loved it so much when he saw it that he died—so folk say—because he could not have it. Much beauty had he, and little wit, but Cliges had greater store of both, just as fine gold surpasses copper, and yet more than I can say. His hair seemed like fine gold and his face a fresh-blown rose. His nose was well shaped, and his mouth beautiful, and he was of great stature as Nature best knew how to frame him; for in him alone she put all at once what she is wont to dole out to each in portions. In framing him Nature was so lavish that she put everything into him all at once and gave him whatsoever she could. Such was Cliges who had in him wisdom and beauty, generosity and strength. He had the timber together with the bark, and knew more of fencing and of archery, of birds and of hounds, than Tristram, King Mark's nephew; not one grace was lacking to Cliges.

Cliges in all his beauty was standing before his uncle; and those who did not know him were in a fever to see him; and also those who do not know the maiden are eagerly straining to see her; all look at her with wonder; but Cliges, in love, directs his eyes to her secretly, and withdraws them so prudently that neither in the going or the coming of the gaze can one consider him a fool for his action. Right lovingly he regards her; but he does not pay heed to the fact that the maiden pays him back in kind. In true love not in flattery he gives his eyes into her keeping, and receives hers. Right good seems this exchange to her; and it would have seemed to her far better if she had known somewhat of his worth. But she knows no more than that she sees him fair; and if she were ever destined to love aught because of the beauty that she might see in it, it is not meet that she should set her heart elsewhere. She has set her eyes and her heart there; and he in his turn has promised her his. Promised? Nay, but given for good and all. Given? Nay, in faith, I lie; he has not, for no one can give his heart. Needs must I say it in a different fashion. I will not speak as they speak who join two hearts in one body; for it is not true, and has not even the semblance of truth to say that one body can have two hearts at once. And even if they could come together such a thing could not be believed. But, and it please you to hearken to me, I shall be able well to render you the reason why two hearts blend in one without coming together. In so far as only they blend in one, the will of each passes from one to the other, and the twain have the same desire, and because they have the same desire, there are folk who are wont to say that each of them possesses both the hearts. But one heart is not in two places. Well may their desire be the same, and yet each, always, his own heart, just as many different men can sing in harmony one song or verse; and I prove to you by this parable that one body cannot have two hearts because one knows the other's will, or because the second knows what the first loves and what he hates. A body cannot have more than one heart any more than the voices which sing in harmony, so that they seem to be but a single voice, can be the voice of one person alone. But it profits me not to dwell on this; for another task demands my care. Henceforth I must speak of the maiden and of Cliges; and ye shall hear of the Duke of Saxony who has sent to Cologne a nephew of his, a mere stripling, who discloses to the emperor what his uncle, the duke, bids him deliver—that the emperor expect not from him truce or peace if he send not to him his daughter; and let not that man feel confident on the way who thinks to take her thence with him; for he will not find the way void of foes; rather will it be right well defended against him if she is not given up to the duke.

Well did the stripling deliver his message, all without pride and without presumption; but he finds none, nor knight nor emperor, to reply to him. When he saw that they were all silent and that they did it from contempt, he is for quitting the court defiantly. But youth and audacity made him challenge Cliges to joust against him ere he departed. They mount to horse in order to tilt; on both sides they count three hundred so were equal in number. The whole palace is empty and deserted; for there remains there neither man nor woman, nor knight nor damsel, who does not go and mount on the palace roof, on to the battlements, and to the windows, to see and behold those who were to tilt. Even the princess has mounted thither, she whom Love had conquered and won to his will. She is seated at a window where she greatly delights to sit because from thence she can see him whom she has hidden in her heart, nor hath she desire to take him away from that hiding-place; for never will she love any save him. But she knows not what is his name nor who he is or of what race nor does it become her to ask; and yet she longs to hear aught whereat her heart may rejoice. Through the window she looks out on the shields where the gold shines, and on those who carry them slung round their necks, and who take delight in the jousting; but her thought and her glance she has wholly set in one direction, for she gives no thought to aught else. She is eager to gaze on Cliges and follows him with her eyes wherever he goes. And he, on his part, tilts strenuously for her before the eyes of all, only that she may hear that he is valiant and very skilful; for in any case it would be meet that she should esteem him for his prowess. He turns himself toward the nephew of the duke who rode apace, breaking many lances and discomfiting the Greeks; but Cliges, who is mightily vexed thereat, presses with all his weight on his stirrups, and rides to strike him so rapidly that the Saxon, in spite of himself, has voided his saddle-bows. There was a great stir as he rose again. The stripling rises and mounts, and thinks to avenge thoroughly his shame; but many a man thinks to avenge his shame if he is permitted, who increases it. The youth rushes towards Cliges; and Cliges lowers his lance to meet him; and attacks him with such violence that he bears him once more to the ground. Now has the youth redoubled his shame, and all his folk are dismayed thereat;

for well they see that never will they leave the fray with honour; for none of them is there so valiant, that if Cliges comes attacking him he can remain in his saddle-bow to meet him. Right glad thereof are they of Germany and they of Greece when they see that their side are sending the Saxons about their business; for the Saxons depart as though discomfited, while the others pursue them with contumely until they catch them up at a stream. Many of the foe do they plunge and immerse therein. Cliges, in the deepest part of the ford, has thrown the duke's nephew, and so many others with him, that to their shame and their vexation, they flee, mournful and sad. But Cliges returns with joy, bearing off the prize for valour on both sides; and he came straight to a door which was close to the place where Fenice was standing who exacts the toll of a sweet look as he enters the door, a toll which he pays her, for their eyes have met. Thus has one conquered the other.

But there is no German whether of the north or of the south so much as able to speak who does not say: "God! who is this in whom so great beauty blooms? God! whence has the power come to him so early that he has won so great distinction?" Thus asks this man and that, "Who is this youth, who is he?" till throughout the city they soon know the truth of it, both his name and his father's, and the promise which the emperor had made and granted to him. It is already so much told and noised abroad that even the maiden hears tell of it, who had great joy in her heart thereat because now she can never say that Love has scorned her, nor can she complain of aught; for he makes her love the fairest, the most courteous, and the most valiant man that one could ever find anywhere; but she must needs have as her husband one who cannot please her; and she is full of anguish and distress thereat; for she does not know with whom to take counsel concerning him whom she desires save only with her own thoughts as she lies awake. And thought and wakefulness so deal with her that they blanch her and altogether change her complexion, so that one can see quite clearly by her loss of colour that she has not what she desires; for she plays less than her wont, and laughs less, and disports herself less; but she hides it well and denies it stoutly if any ask what ails her. Her nurse, who had brought her up from infancy, was named Thessala, and was versed in the black art. She was called Thessala because she was born in Thessaly where sorceries are made, taught, and practised; for the women who are of that country make charms and enchantments.

Thessala sees that she whom Love has in his power is wan and pale, and she has addressed her secretly. "God!" quoth she, "are you enchanted, my sweet lady dear, that you have so wan a countenance? Much do I wonder what ails you. Tell me, if you know, in what part this sickness possesses you most; for if any one can cure you of it you can rely on me, for well can I give you back your health. Well know I how to cure a man of dropsy, and I know how to cure of gout, of quinsy, and of asthma; I know so much about the water and so much about the pulse that evil would be the hour in which you would take another leech. And I know, if I dared say it, of enchantments and of charms, well proven and true, more than ever Medea knew. Never spake I a word of it to you; and yet I have brought you up till now; but never reproach yourself at all for it, for never would I have said aught to you if I had not seen for a surety that such a malady has attacked you, that you have need of my aid. Lady, tell me your malady, and you will act wisely in doing so before it gets further hold of you. The emperor has set me in charge of you that I may take care of you; and I have given such diligence that I have kept you in sound health. Now shall I have lost my pains if I heal you not of this ill. Beware that you hide it not from me, be it illness or aught else." The maiden dares not openly disclose her whole desire because she is greatly afeard that Thessala may blame and dissuade her. And yet because she hears her greatly vaunt and extol herself, and say that she is learned in enchantment, in charms and potions, she will tell her what is her case, why her face is pale and wan; but beforehand she will make her promise that she will hide it for ever and will never dissuade her.

"Nurse," quoth she, "of a truth I thought that I felt no ill; but I shall speedily think that I am sick. The mere fact of my thinking of it causes me much ill and eke alarms me. But how does one know unless he put it to the test what may be good and what ill? My ill differs from all other ills; for—and I be willing to tell you the truth of it—much it joys me, and much it grieves me, and I delight in my discomfort; and if there can be a disease which gives pleasure, my sorrow is my desire, and my grief is my health. I know not then whereof I should complain; for I know nought whence evil may come to me if it come not from my desire. Possibly my desire is a malady; but I take so much pleasure in that desire that it causes me a pleasant grief; and I have so much joy in my sorrow that my malady is a pleasant one. Thessala, nurse! tell me now, is not this sorrow which seems sweet to me, and yet which tortures me, a deceitful one? I know not how I may recognise whether it be an infirmity or no. Nurse! tell me now the name, and the manner, and the nature, of it. But be well assured that I have no care to recover in any wise, for I cherish the anguish of it exceedingly." Thessala, who was right wise as regards Love and all his ways, knows and understands by her speech that that which distracts her proceeds from Love—because she calls and names it sweet—it is certain that she loves; for all other ills are bitter save that alone which comes from loving; but Love transmutes its own bitterness into pleasure, and sweetness often turns to its opposite. But Thessala, who well knew the matter, replies to her: "Fear nought, I will tell you well both the nature and the name of your disease. You have told me, methinks, that the pain which you feel seems to you to be joy and health: of such a nature is love-sickness; for there is in it joy and sweetness. Therefore I prove to you that you love; for I find pleasure in no sickness save only in love-sickness. All other ills as a rule are always grievous and horrible; but Love is pleasant and tranquil. You love; I am fully certain of it. I regard it not as base in you; but I will hold it baseness if through childishness or folly you conceal your heart from me." "Nurse, truly you are talking to no purpose; for first I mean to be certain and sure that never by any chance will you speak thereof to any living creature." "Lady, certainly the winds will speak of it sooner than I unless you give me permission; and of this I will make you sure—that I will help you with regard to this matter, so that you may know of a surety, that by me you will have your joy." "Nurse, in that case you would have cured me; but the emperor is giving me in marriage whereat I am grievously afflicted and sad because he who pleases me is nephew of him whom I am to wed. And if this man have his joy of me, then have I lost mine; and there is no more joy to be looked for. Rather would I be torn limb from limb than that the love of Iseult and of Tristram should be renewed in the case of us twain; for of them are such mad actions told that I am ashamed to recount them. I could not reconcile myself to the life that Iseult led. Love in her became exceeding base; for her body belonged to two masters and her heart entirely to one. Thus she spent her whole life; for she never refused the two. Reason was there none in this love; but mine is ever constant; and at no cost will a partition ever be made of my body or of my heart. Never of a truth shall my body be debased; never shall there be two partners of it. Let him who owns the heart have the body also; he excludes all others from it. But this I cannot know—how he to whom my heart yields itself can have my body since my father is giving me to another; and I dare not gainsay him. And when he shall be lord of my body if he do aught with it that I do not wish, it is not meet that it welcome another. Moreover, this man cannot wed wife without breaking faith; but if he wrong not his nephew, Cliges will have the empire after his death. But if you can contrive by your arts, that this man to whom I am given and pledged might never have part or lot in me, you would have done me good service according to my will. Nurse, prithee strive that this man break not his faith; for he gave his pledge to the father of Cliges, promising just as Alexander had made him swear, that never would he take wedded wife. His pledge is about to be broken, for straightway he intends to wed me. But I cherish Cliges so dearly that I would rather be buried than that he should lose through me a farthing of the inheritance which ought to be his. May never child be born of me by whom he may be disinherited! Nurse, now bestir yourself in the matter that I may be yours for ever." Then her nurse tells her and assures her that she will weave such spells and potions and enchantments that she would be ill-advised to have concern or fear for this emperor; so soon as he shall have drunk of the potion that she will give him to drink, and they will both lie together; but however close she will be to him, she can be as secure as if there were a wall between the two of them. "But let not this and this only vex you if he has his pleasure of you in dreams; for, when he shall be sound asleep, he will have joy of you in dreaming; and will quite surely think that he has his joy of you waking, nor will he imagine that it is a dream, or vision, or falsehood. He will delight in you so that he will think he is awake while he is sleeping."

The maiden loves and approves and esteems this boon and this service. Her nurse, who promises her this, and vows to keep faith with her, puts her in good hope; for by this means she will think to come to her joy however long she have to wait. For never will Cliges be so ill-disposed to her—if he knows that he loves him; and for his sake lives so as to guard her maidenhead in order to shield for him his inheritance—as not to have some pity on her if he prove himself of a noble stock, and if he is such as he ought to be. The maiden believes her nurse, and trusts and confides in her greatly. The one vows and swears to the other that this plan will be kept so secret that never will it be known in the future. Thus the parley is ended; and when it came to the morning the emperor of Germany sends for his daughter. She comes at his command—but why should I spin out my story? The two emperors together have so arranged matters that the marriage takes place and joy begins in the palace. But I will not delay to speak of each thing severally. I will turn my tale of Thessala, who does not cease to make and mix potions.

Thessala crushes her potion; she puts therein spices in plenty for sweetening and blending. Well does she pound and mix it, and strains it till the whole is clear, and there is nought acid nor bitter there; for the spices which are in it make it sweet and of pleasant odour. When the potion was prepared, then had the day run its course, and the tables were placed for supper, and the tablecloths laid; but she delays the supper. It is Thessala's task to spy out by what device, by what messenger, she will send her potion. They were all seated at the banquet; they had had more than six courses and Cliges was serving his uncle. Thessala, who sees him serve, reflects that he is wasting his Service; for he is serving to his own disinheritance, and this is a great sorrow and anxiety to her. Then like the courteous dame that she is, she bethinks herself that she will make him to whom it will be joy and profit serve the potion. Thessala sends for Cliges, and he went straightway to her, and has inquired, and asked of her why she had sent for him. "Friend," quoth she, "at this banquet I wish to pay the emperor the flattering meed of a potion that he will greatly esteem. I will not that he drink to-night, either at supper or at bedtime, of any other drink. I think that it will give him much pleasure; for never did he taste of aught so good nor did any beverage ever cost so much; and take good care—I warn you of this—that no other drink of it because there is too little of it for that. And, moreover, I give you this advice, that he never know whence it came; but let him think it came by accident, that you found it among the presents, and that because you tested it, and perceived by the scent of its bouquet the fragrance of good spices, and because you saw that it sparkled, you poured the wine into his cup. If by chance he inquire of it, that will doubtless be the end of the matter. But have no evil suspicion anent aught that I have said; for the beverage is pure and wholesome, and full of good spices, and it may be, as I think, that at some future time it will make you blithe." When he hears that good will come of it he takes the potion and goes away; for he knows not that there is aught wrong. In a cup of crystal he has set it before the emperor. The emperor has taken the cup, for he has great trust in his nephew. He drinks a mighty draught of the potion; and now he feels the virtue of it; for it penetrates from the head to the heart, and from the heart it returns to his head, and it permeates him again and again. It saturates his whole body without hurting him. And by the time the tables were removed, the emperor had drunk so much of the beverage which had pleased him, that never will he get free of it. Each night while asleep he will be intoxicated; and yet it will excite him so much that though asleep, he will dream that he is awake.

Now is the emperor mocked. Many bishops and abbots there were at the benediction and consecration of the bed. When it was bedtime the emperor, as it behoved him, lay with his wife that night. "As it behoved him"—therein have I lied, for he never embraced or touched her though they lay together in one bed. At first the maiden trembles; for greatly does she fear and feel alarm lest the potion take no effect. But it has so bewitched him that never will he have his will of her or of another save when asleep. But then he will have such ecstasy as one can have in dreaming; and yet he will hold the dream for true. In one word I have told you all: never had he other delight of her than in dreams. Thus must he needs fare evermore if he can lead his bride away; but before he can hold her in safety a great disaster, I ween, may befall him. For when he will return home, the duke, to whom she was first given, will be no laggard. The duke has gathered a great force, and has occupied all the marches, and his spies are at the court, and inform him each day of all he wants to know, and tell him all the measures he must take, and how long they will tarry, and when they will return, through what places, and by what passes. The emperor did not long tarry after the wedding. Blithely he departs from Cologne; and the emperor of Germany escorts him with a very great company because he greatly fears and dreads the might of the Duke of Saxony.

The two emperors proceed and stop not till they reach Ratisbon; and on one evening they were lodged by the Danube in the meadow. The Greeks were in their tents in the meadows beside the Black Forest. The Saxons who were observing them were encamped opposite them. The duke's nephew was left all alone on a hill to keep a look-out, and see whether, peradventure, he might gain any advantage over those yonder or wreak any mischief upon them.

From his post of vantage he saw Cliges riding with three other striplings who were taking their pleasure, carrying lances and shields in order to tilt and to disport themselves. Now is the duke's nephew bent on attacking and injuring them if ever he can. With five comrades he sets out; and the six have posted themselves secretly beside the wood in a valley, so that the Greeks never saw them till they issued from the valley, and till the duke's nephew rushes upon Cliges and strikes him, so that he wounds him a little in the region of the spine. Cliges stoops and bows his head, so that the lance glances off him; nevertheless, it wounds him a little.

When Cliges perceives that he is wounded he has rushed upon the stripling, and strikes him straightway with such violence that he thrusts his lance right through his heart and fells him dead. Then the Saxons, who fear him mightily, all take to flight and scatter through the heart of the forest while Cliges, who knows not of the ambush, commits a reckless and foolish act; for he separates himself from his comrades, and pursues in that direction in which the duke's force was. And now all the host were preparing to make an attack on the Greeks. Cliges, all alone, without aid, pursues them; and the youths all dismayed because of their lord whom they have lost, come running into the duke's presence; and, weeping, recount to him the evil hap of his nephew. The duke thinks it no light matter; by God and all his saints, he swears that never in all his life will he have joy or good luck as long as he shall know that the slayer of his nephew is alive. He says that he who will bring him Cliges' head shall verily be deemed his friend, and will give him great comfort. Then a knight has boasted that the head of Cliges will be offered to the duke by him; let the duke but rely on him.

Cliges pursues the youths till he swooped down on the Saxons, and is seen by the knight who has engaged to carry off his head. Straightway, that knight departs and stays no longer. But Cliges has retreated in order to elude his enemies; and he returned at full gallop thither where he had left his comrades. But he has found none of them there; for they had returned to the tents to relate their adventure. And the emperor summoned Greeks and Germans alike to horse. Through all the host the barons speedily arm themselves and mount. But the Saxon knight, all armed, his visor laced, has continued to pursue Cliges at a gallop. Cliges, who never wished to have aught in common with a recreant or coward, sees him come alone. First of all the knight has assailed him with words: he stoutly calls him baseborn fellow, for he could not conceal the mind he had of him. "Fellow," quoth he, "here wilt thou leave the forfeit for my lord, whom thou hast slain. If I bear not off thy head with me, then esteem me not worth a bad Byzantine coin. I will to make the duke a present of it, for I will not accept any other forfeit in its stead. So much will I render to him for his nephew; and he will have had a good exchange for him." Cliges hears that the Saxon is abusing him as a madman and low-bred fellow. "Man," quoth he, "now defend yourself; for I defy you to take my head, and you shall not have it without my leave." Forthwith the one seeks the other. The Saxon has missed his stroke; and Cliges thrusts so hard that he made man and steed fall all in a heap. The steed falls backwards on his rider with such violence that it completely breaks one of his legs. Cliges dismounts on the green grass and disarms him. When he had disarmed him, then he dons the arms himself, and has cut off his head with the victim's own sword. When he had cut off his head, he has fixed it on to the point of his lance; and says that he will present it to the duke to whom his enemy had vowed to present Cliges' own head if he could meet him in the fight. No sooner had Cliges placed the helmet on his head, taken the shield, (not his own, but the shield of him who had fought with him), and no sooner had he mounted on the foeman's horse, leaving his own rider-less in order to dismay the Greeks, than he saw more than a hundred banners and battalions, great and fully equipped, of Greeks and Germans mingled. Now will begin a very fierce and cruel melee between the Saxons and the Greeks. As soon as Cliges sees them come, he goes straight towards the Saxons; and the Greeks exert themselves to pursue him; for on account of his arms they do not know him; and his uncle, who sees the head that he is bringing, is marvellously discomforted thereat. No wonder is it if he fears for his nephew. The whole host musters in his wake; and Cliges lets them pursue him in order to begin the melee till the Saxons perceive him coming; but the arms with which he is clad and furnished mislead them all. He has mocked at them and scorned them; for the duke and all the others as he advanced with hoisted lance, say: "Our knight is coming! On the point of the lance that he holds he is bringing the head of Cliges; and the Greeks follow after him. Now to horse to succour him!" Then they all give the rein to their horses; and Cliges spurs towards the Saxons, covering himself behind his shield and doubling himself up, his lance upright, the head on its point. Not one whit less courage than a lion had he, though he was no stronger than another. On both sides they believe that he is dead—Saxons, and Greeks and Germans—and the one side are blithe thereat; and the other side, grieved; but soon will the truth be known. For now has Cliges no longer held his peace: shouting, he gallops towards a Saxon, and strikes him with his ashen lance with the head on it, full in the breast, so that he has lost his stirrups; and he calls out, "Barons, strike! I am Cliges whom you seek. On now, bold freeborn knights! Let there be no coward, for ours is the first shock. Let no craven taste of such a dainty dish."

The emperor greatly rejoiced when he heard his nephew, Cliges, who thus addresses and exhorts them; right glad and comforted is he thereof. And the duke is utterly dumfounded, for now he knows well that he is betrayed unless his force is the greater; he bids his men close their ranks and keep together. And the Greeks, in close array, have not gone far from them, for now they are spurring and pricking. On both sides they couch their lances and meet and receive each other as it behoved them to do in such a fight. At the first encounter, they pierce shields and shatter lances, cut girths, break stirrups; the steeds stand bereft of those who fall upon the field. But no matter what the others do, Cliges and the duke meet; they hold their lances couched; and each strikes the other on his shield with so great valour that the lances, which were strong and well wrought, break into splinters. Cliges was a skilful horseman: he remained upright in his saddle, never stumbling nor wavering. The duke has lost his saddle, and in spite of himself has voided the saddle-bows. Cliges thinks to take him and lead him away captive, and mightily toils and strains; but the strength he needed was not his. For the Saxons were all around, and they rescue their duke by force. Nevertheless, Cliges leaves the field without injury; with a prize; for he leads away the duke's steed which was whiter than wool and which, for the use of a man of valour, was worth all the possessions of Octavian of Rome: the steed was an Arab one. Great joy manifest Greeks and Germans when they see Cliges mounted on it; for they had seen the worth and the perfection of the Arab; but they did not suspect an ambush nor will they ever perceive it till they receive great loss therefrom.

A spy has come to the duke with news at which he has waxed full joyous. "Duke," quoth the spy, "no man has been left in all the tents of the Greeks who can defend himself. Now can thy men take the daughter of the emperor, if thou wilt trust my words, while thou seest the Greeks desperately bent on the fight and on the battle. Give me a hundred of thy knights and I will give them thy lady-love. By an old and lonely path, I will lead them so prudently that they shall not be seen or met by Saxon or German till they will be able to take the maiden in her tent, and lead her away so unhindered that never will she be denied them." The duke is blithe at this thing. He has sent a hundred and more wise knights with the spy; and the spy has led them in such wise that they take the maiden as a prize, nor have they spent great force thereon, for easily were they able to lead her away. When they had taken her some distance from the tents, they sent her away attended by twelve of them, nor did the rest accompany the twelve far. Twelve of them lead away the maiden; the others have told the duke the news of their success. Nought else was there that the duke had desired, and straightway he makes a truce with the Greeks till the morrow. They have given and accepted a truce. The duke's men have returned; and the Greeks without any delay return, each one to his tent. But Cliges remained alone on a hill so that no one noticed him till he saw the twelve coming, and the damsel whom they were taking away at full speed and at a gallop. Cliges, who longs to gain renown, forthwith dashes in their direction, for he thinks to himself, and his heart tells him that it is not for nothing they are fleeing. The very moment that he saw them, he dashes after them; and they see him; but they think and believe a foolish thing. "The duke is following us," each one says, "let us wait for him a little; for he has left the host unattended and is coming after us very swiftly." There is not a single one who does not believe this. They all desire to go to meet him; but each desires to go alone. Cliges must needs descend into a great valley between two mountains. Never would he have recognised their insignia if they had not come to meet him, or if they had not awaited him. Six of them advanced to meet him; but soon will they have had an ill meeting with him. The others stay with the maiden and lead her on, gently, at a walking pace. And the six go at full speed, spurring incessantly through the valley. He who had the swiftest horse outstripped all the rest, crying aloud: "Duke of Saxony! God preserve thee! Duke! We have regained thy lady. Now shall the Greeks never carry her off; for she will now be given and handed over to thee." When Cliges has heard these words that the other cries out, no smile had he in his heart; rather is it a marvel that frenzy does not seize him. Never was any wild beast: leopardess, or tigress, or lioness, who sees her young taken, so embittered, and furious, and lusting, for the fight as was Cliges who cares not to live if he fail his lady. Rather would he die than not have her. Very great wrath has he for this calamity and exceeding great courage does it give him. He spurs and pricks the Arab; and goes to deal the blazoned shield of the Saxon such a blow that—I lie not—he made him feel the lance at his heart. This has given Cliges confidence. More than a full acre's measure has he spurred and pricked the Arab before the second has drawn near, for they came, one by one. The one has no fear for the other; for he fights with each singly and meets them one by one, nor has the one aid of the other. He makes an attack on the second, who thought to tell the supposed duke news of Cliges' discomfiture, and to rejoice thereat as the first had done. But Cliges recks little of words or of listening to his discourse. He proceeds to thrust his lance in his body so that when he draws it out again the blood gushes out; and he bereaves his foe of life and speech. After the two, he joins issue with a third who thinks to find him overjoyed and to gladden him with news of his own discomfiture. He came spurring against him; but before he has the chance to say a word, Cliges has thrust his lance a fathom deep into his body. To the fourth he gives such a blow on the neck, that he leaves him in a swoon on the field. After the fourth, he gallops against the fifth, and then after the fifth, against the sixth. Of these, none stood his ground against him; rather does Cliges leave them all silent and dumb. Still less has he feared and more boldly sought the rest of them. After this has he no concern about these six.

When he was free from care as regards these, he goes to make a present of shame and of misfortune to the rest who are escorting the maiden. He has overtaken them, and attacks them like a wolf, who famished and fasting rushes on his prey. Now seems it to him that he was born in a good hour, since he can display his chivalry and courage before her who is all his life. Now is he dead if he free her not; and she, on the other hand, is likewise dead; for she is greatly discomforted for him, but does not know that he is so near her. Cliges, with feutred lance, has made a charge which pleased her; and he strikes one Saxon and then another so that with one single charge he has made them both bite the dust, and splinters his ashen lance. The foemen fall in such anguish that they have no power to rise again to hurt or molest him, for they were sore wounded in their bodies. The other four, in great wrath, go all together to strike Cliges; but he neither stumbles nor trembles nor have they unhorsed him. Swiftly he snatches from the scabbard his sword of sharpened Steel; and that she who awaits his love may be right grateful to him, he encounters with lightning swiftness a Saxon, and strikes him with his sharp sword, so that he has severed from his trunk, his head and half his neck: no tenderer pity had he for him. Fenice, who watches and beholds, knows not that it is Cliges. Fain would she that it were he; but because there is danger she says to herself that she would not wish it. For two reasons is she his good friend; for she fears his death and desires his honour. And Cliges receives at the sword's point the three who offer him fierce combat; they pierce and cleave his shield, but they cannot get him into their power or cleave the links of his shirt of mail. And nought that Cliges can reach stands firm before his blow; for he cleaves and breaks asunder all; he wheels round more quickly than the top which is urged on and driven by the whip. Prowess and love entwine him and make him bold and keen in fight. He has dealt so grievously with the Saxons that he has killed or conquered them all, wounded some, and killed others; but he let one of them escape because they were a match, one for the other, and so that, by him, the duke might know his loss and mourn. But before this man left him, he prevailed upon Cliges to tell him his name; and went for his part to tell it to the duke, who had great wrath thereat. Now the duke hears of his misfortune, and had great grief and great care thereat. And Cliges leads away Fenice, who thrills and tortures him with the pangs of love; but if now he does not hear her confession, long time will love be adverse to him; and also to her if she, on her side, is silent and say not her will; for now in the hearing, one of the other, can they reveal their inmost hearts. But so much do they fear refusal that they dare not betray their hearts. He fears that she might reject him; she, on her part, would have betrayed herself if she had not feared rejection. And, nevertheless, the one betrays his thoughts to the other with the eyes if they could only have known it. They speak by glances with their eyes; but they are so craven with their tongues that in no wise dare they speak of the love which masters them. If she dare not begin it, it is no marvel; for a maiden ought to be a simple and shy creature. But why does he wait; and why does he delay, who is thoroughly bold in her behalf, and has shown dread of none but her? God! Whence comes this fear to him that he fears a single maiden, weak and timid, simple and shy? At this, methinks, I see dogs fleeing before the hare, and the fish hunting the beaver, the lamb the wolf, the dove the eagle. So would it be if the villein were to flee before his hoe by which he gains his livelihood, and with which he toils. So would it be if the falcon were to flee from the duck, and the gerfalcon from the heron, and the great pike from the minnow, and if the stag were to chase the lion; so do things go topsy-turvy. But a desire comes upon me to give some reason why it happens to true lovers, that wit and courage fail them to express what they have in their thoughts when they have leisure and opportunity and time.

You who are being instructed in Love, who faithfully uphold the customs and rites of his court, and who never broke his law whatever might have befallen you for your obedience, tell me if one can see anything which affords Love's delight but that lovers shiver and grow pale thereat. Never shall there be a man opposed to me that I do not convince of this; for he who does not grow pale and shiver thereat, who does not lose wit and memory like a thief, pursues and seeks that which is not fittingly his. A servant who does not fear his lord, ought not to stay in his retinue or serve him. He who does not esteem his lord, does not fear him; and he who does not esteem him, does not hold him dear; but rather seeks to cheat him and to pilfer somewhat of his property. For fear ought a servant to tremble when his lord calls him or sends for him. And he who commends himself to Love makes Love his master and his lord; and it is meet that he have him in Reverence; and greatly fear and honour him if he wishes to stand well with his court. Love without fear and without dread is fire without flame and without heat; daylight without sun; honeycomb without honey; summer without flowers; winter without frost; sky without moon; a book without letters. Thus do I wish to refute such an opponent; for where fear is lacking there is no love worth mentioning. It behoves him who wishes to love to fear also; for if he does not he cannot love; but let him fear her only whom he loves; and in her behoof let him be thoroughly bold. Therefore, Cliges commits no fault or wrong if he fears his lady-love. But for this fear he would not have failed forthwith to have spoken to her of love and sought her love, however the matter had happed if she had not been his uncle's wife. For this cause his wound rankles in him; and it pains and grieves him the more because he dare not say what he yearns to say.

Thus they return towards their company; and if they talk of anything, there was in their talk nothing about which they cared. Each sat on a white horse; and they rode quickly towards the army where there was great lamentation. Throughout the host they are beside themselves with grief; but they hit upon an untrue saying when they say that Cliges is dead — thereat is the mourning very great and loud. And they fear for Fenice; they deem not that they will ever have her again; and both for her and for him the whole host is in very great sorrow. But these two will not delay much longer; and the whole state of matters will take a different appearance; for already they have returned to the host and have turned the sorrow into joy. Joy returns and sorrow flies. They all come to meet them so that the whole host assembles. The two emperors together, when they heard the news about Cliges and about the maiden, go to meet them with very great joy; but each one longs to hear how Cliges had found and rescued the lady. Cliges tells them the tale; and those who hear it marvel greatly Thereat; and much do they praise his prowess and valour. But on the other side the duke, who swears and protests, is furious; and declares that if Cliges dares there shall be a single combat between the two of them; and that he will order matters in such wise, that if Cliges wins the combat, the emperor shall go away in safety, and take the maiden unhindered; but that if he kills or conquers Cliges, who has done him many an injury, let there for this be neither truce nor peace till after each has done his utmost. This the duke essays; and through an interpreter of his, who knew Greek and German, gives the two emperors to know that thus he wishes to have the battle.

The messenger delivers his message in one and the other language so well that all understood. The whole host resounds and is in an uproar about it; and men say, that never may it please God, that Cliges fight the battle; and both the emperors are in a very great alarm thereat; but Cliges falls at their feet and prays them let it not grieve them; but that, if ever he has done aught that has pleased them, he may have this battle as a guerdon and as a reward. And if it is denied him never will he for a single day be a blessing and an honour to his uncle. The emperor, who held his nephew as dear as duty bade him, with his hand raises him up from his knees and says:

"Fair nephew, greatly does it grieve me that I know you to be so wedded to fighting; for after joy I expect sorrow therefrom. You have made me glad; I cannot deny it; but much it grieves me to grant this boon and send you to the battle; for that I see you yet too young. And I know you to be of such proud courage that in no wise dare I deny anything that it please you to ask; for know well that it would be done but to please you; but if my prayer availed aught, never would you take on you this burden." "Sire, you are pleading in vain," quoth Cliges, "for may God confound me if I would accept the whole world on condition that I did not fight this battle. I know not why I should seek from you a long respite or a long delay." The emperor weeps with pity, and Cliges, on his side, weeps with joy when he grants him the battle. There had he wept many a joyful tear, nor had he secured delay, nor limit of time, before it was the hour of Prime; by his own messenger was the battle announced to the duke, just as he had demanded it.

The duke, who thinks and believes and imagines that Cliges will not be able to defend himself against him, but that he will soon have slain or conquered him, quickly has himself armed. Cliges, who is longing for the battle, thinks that he need have no care as to how to defend himself against the duke. He asks the emperor for arms, and prays him to dub him knight; and, of his grace, the emperor gives him arms and Cliges takes them; for his heart is enamoured of the battle and much does he desire and long for it. He hastens full swiftly to arm himself; when he was armed from head to foot, the emperor, who was full of anxiety, goes to gird the sword on his side. Cliges mounts on the white Arab, fully armed; from his neck he hangs by the straps a shield made of elephant's bone, such that it will neither break nor split nor had it blazon or device; the armour was all white, and the steed and the harness were all whiter than any snow.

Cliges and the duke are armed, and the one has announced to the other that they will meet half-way, and that, on both sides, their men shall all be without swords and without lances, bound by oaths and their word of honour that never, as long as the combat shall last, will there be any so bold as to dare to move for any reason, any more than he would dare to pluck out his own eye. Bound by this covenant they have met, and the delay has seemed very long to each champion; for each thinks to have the glory and the joy of victory. But before there was a blow struck, the maiden, who is much concerned for Cliges, has herself escorted thither; but on this is she quite resolved: that if he dies, she will die. Never will any hope of consolation avail to deter her from dying with him; for without him life has no charm for her.

When all had come into the field, high and low, young and hoary, and the guards bad been set there, then have both champions taken their lances; and they meet in no half-hearted way, so that each breaks his lance, and both are unhorsed and fail to keep their saddles. But quickly have they risen to their feet, for they were not at all wounded, and again they encounter without delay. They play a merry tune with their swords on the resounding helms, so that their retinue are amazed; and it seems to those who watch them that the helmets are on fire and ablaze. And when the swords rebound, glowing sparks jet forth as from red-hot iron which the smith hammers on the anvil when he draws it from the furnace. Very lavish are both the warriors in dealing blows in great Store; and each has a good will to pay back quickly what he borrows; neither the one nor the other ceases from paying back capital and interest immediately, all without count and without stint. But the duke comes on in great anger, and right wroth and furious is he because he has not quelled and slain Cliges at the first encounter. He deals him a great blow, marvellous and strong, such that at his feet Cliges has fallen on one knee.

At the blow whereby Cliges fell was the emperor much amazed; he was no whit less bewildered than if he had been behind the shield himself. Then Fenice, so much was she amazed, can no longer restrain herself, whatever might come of it, from crying: "God! Aid!" as loud as ever she could. But she had called out but one word when, forthwith, her voice failed, and she fell swooning, and with arms outstretched so that her face was a little wounded. Two noble barons raised her, and have held her on her feet till she has returned to her senses. But never did any who saw her, whatever appearance she presented, know why she swooned. Never did any man blame her for it; rather they have all praised her; for there is not a single one who does not believe that she would have done the same for his sake if he had been in Cliges' place; but in all this there is no truth. Cliges, when Fenice cried, heard and marked her right well. The sound restored to him strength and courage, and be springs swiftly to his feet, and advanced furiously to meet the duke, and thrusts at him, and presses him so that the duke was amazed thereat; for he finds him more greedy for combat, more strong and agile than he had found him before, it seems to him, when they first encountered. And because he fears his onset he says to him: "Knight, so may God save me, I see thee right courageous and valiant. But if it had not been for my nephew, whom I shall never forget, willingly would I have made peace with thee, and would have released thee from the quarrel; for never would I have meddled any more in the matter." "Duke," says Cliges, "what may be your pleasure? Is it not meet that he who cannot make good his claim yield it, one of two evils; when one has to choose, one ought to choose the lesser. When your nephew picked a quarrel with me, he acted unwisely. I will serve you in the same way—be assured of it—if I ever can, if I do not receive submission from you." The duke, to whom it seems that Cliges was growing in strength every moment, thinks that it is much better for him to stop short half-way before he is altogether wearied out. Nevertheless, he does not confess to him the truth quite openly, but he says: "Knight, I see thee debonair and agile and of great courage. But exceeding young art thou: for this reason I reflect, and I know of a surety, that if I conquer and kill thee, never should I win praise or esteem thereby, nor should I ever see any man of valour in whose hearing I should dare to confess that I had fought with thee, for I should do honour to thee and shame to myself. But if those knowst what honour means, a great honour will it be to thee for ever that thou hast stood thy ground against me, even for two encounters only. Now a wish and desire has come to me, to release thee from the quarrel and not to fight with thee any longer." "Duke," quoth Cliges, "you talk idly. You shall say it aloud in the hearing of all, and never shall it be told or related that you have done me a kindness, or that you have had mercy on me. In the hearing of one and all of these who are here, you will have to declare it if you wish to make peace with me." The duke declares it in the hearing of all. Thus have they made peace and agreement; but whatever the issue of the matter, Cliges had the honour and the renown of it; and the Greeks had very great joy thereof. But the Saxons could not make light of the matter; for well had they all seen their lord exhausted and worsted; nor is there any question but that, if he had been able to do better for himself, this peace would never have been made; rather would he have rent the soul out of Cliges' body if he had been able to do it.

The duke returns to Saxony, grieved and downcast and Ashamed; for of his men—there are not two who do not hold him a conquered man, a craven, and a coward. The Saxons, with all their shame, have returned to Saxony. And the Greeks delay no longer; they return towards Constantinople with great joy and with great gladness; for well by his prowess has Cliges assured to them the way. Now the emperor of Germany no further follows or attends them. After taking leave of the Greek folk and of his daughter and of Cliges and of the emperor, he has remained in Germany; and the emperor of the Greeks goes away right glad and right joyful. Cliges, the valiant, the well-bred, thinks of his father's command. If his uncle the emperor will grant him leave, he will go to request and pray him to let him go to Britain to speak to his uncle the king; for he craves to know and see him. He sets out for the presence of the emperor, and begs him if it please him to let him go to Britain to see his uncle and his friends. Very gently has he made this request; but his uncle refuses it to him when he has heard and listened to the whole of his request and his story. "Fair nephew," quoth he, "it pleases me not that you should wish to leave me. Never will I give you this leave or this permission without great grief; for right pleasant and convenient is it that you should be my partner and co-ruler with me of all my empire."

Now there is nothing which pleases Cliges, since his uncle denies him what he asks and requests; and he says: "Fair Sire, it becomes me not, nor am I brave or wise enough to be given this partnership with you or with another so as to rule an empire; very young am I and know but little. For this reason is gold applied to the touchstone because one wishes to know if it is real gold. So wish I—that is the end and sum of it—to assay and prove myself where I think to find the touchstone. In Britain if I am valiant I shall be able to put myself to the touch with the Whetstone; and with the true and genuine assay by which I shall test my prowess. In Britain are those valiant men of whom honour and prowess boast. And he who wishes to gain honour, ought to join himself to their company; for there the honour resides and is won which appertains to the man of valour. Therefore, I ask you this leave; and know of a surety that if you do not send me thither and do not grant me the boon, then I shall go without your leave." "Fair nephew, rather do I give it you freely when I see you thus minded; for I would not have the heart to detain you by force or by prayer. Now may God give you heart and will to return soon since neither prayer nor prohibition nor force could prevail in the matter. I would have you take with you a talent of gold and of silver, and horses to delight you will I give you, all at your choice." No sooner had he said his word than Cliges has bowed to him. All whatsoever the emperor has devised and promised was at once set before him. Cliges took as much wealth and as many comrades as pleased and behoved him; but for his own private use he takes away four different steeds: one white, one sorrel, one dun, one black. But I was about to pass over one thing that must not be omitted. Cliges goes to take leave of Fenice, his lady-love, and to ask her leave to depart; for he would fain commend her to God. He comes before her and kneels down, weeping, so that he moistens with his tears all his tunic and his ermine, and he bends his eyes to the ground; for he dares not look straight in front of him, just as if he has committed some wrong and crime towards her, and now shows by his mien that he has shame for it. And Fenice, who beholds him timidly and shyly, knows not what matter brings him; and she has said to him in some distress: "Friend, fair sir, rise; sit by my side; weep no more and tell me your pleasure." "Lady! What shall I say? What conceal? I seek your permission to depart." "Depart? Why?"

"Lady! I must go away to Britain." "Tell me, then, on what quest, before I give you permission." "Lady, my father, when he died and departed this life, prayed me on no account to fail to go to Britain as soon as I should be a knight. For nothing in the world would I neglect his command. It will behove me not to play the laggard as I go thither. It is a very long journey from here to Greece; and if I were to go thither the journey from Constantinople to Britain would be very long for me. But it is meet that I take leave of you as being the lady whose I am wholly." Many hidden and secret sighs and sobs had he made on setting out; but no one had eyes so wide open or such good hearing as to be able to perceive for a certainty from hearing or sight, that there was love between the twain. Cliges, grievous though it be to him, departs as soon as it is allowed him. He goes away lost in thought; lost in thought remains the emperor and many another; but Fenice is the most pensive of all: she discovers neither bottom nor bound to the thought with which she is filled, so greatly does it overflow and multiply in her. Full of thought she has come to Greece: there was she held in great honour as lady and empress; but her heart and spirit are with Cliges wherever he turns, nor ever seeks she that her heart may return to her unless he bring it back to her, he who is dying of the malady with which he has slain her. And if he recovers, she will recover; never will he pay dear for it unless she too pay dear. Her malady appears in her complexion; for much has she changed and pale has she grown. The fresh, clear, pure hue that Nature had bestowed has wholly deserted her face. Often she weeps, often sighs: little recks she of her empire and of the wealth she has. She has always in her memory the hour that Cliges departed, the farewell that he took of her, how he changed countenance, how he blanched, his tears and his mien, for he came to weep before her, humble, lowly, and on his knees, as if he must needs worship her. All this is pleasant and sweet for her to recall and to retrace. Then to provide herself with a luscious morsel, she takes on her tongue in lieu of spice a sweet word; and for all Greece she would not wish that he who said that word should, in the sense in which she took it, have intended deceit; for she lives on no other dainty nor does aught else please her. This word alone sustains and feeds her and soothes for her all her suffering. She seeks not to feed herself or quench her thirst with any other meat or drink; for when it came to the parting, Cliges said that he was "wholly hers". This word is so sweet and good to her, that from the tongue it goes to her heart; and she stores it in her heart as well as in her mouth, that she may be the surer of it. She dares not hide this treasure behind any other lock; and she would never be able to store it elsewhere so well as in her heart. In no wise will she ever take it thence so much she fears thieves and robbers; but it is without reason that this fear comes to her; and without reason that she fears birds of prey, for this possession is immovable; rather is it like a building which cannot be destroyed by flood or by fire, and which will never move from its place. But this she knows not, and hence she gives herself agony and pain to seek out and learn something on which she can lay hold; for in divers fashions does she explain it. She holds debate within herself; and makes such replies as these: "With what intention did Cliges say to me 'I am wholly yours' if love did not cause him to say it? With what power of mine can I sway him, that he should esteem me so highly as to make me his lady? Is he not fairer than I, of much nobler birth than I? I see nought but his love that can bestow on me this gift. From my own case, for I cannot evade the scrutiny, I will prove, that if he had not loved me he would never have called himself wholly mine; for just as I could not be wholly his, nor could in honour say so if love had not drawn me to him, so Cliges, on his side, could not in any wise have said that he was wholly mine if love has him not in his bonds. For if he loves me not, he fears me not. Love, which gives me wholly to him, perhaps, gives him wholly to me; but this thought quite dismays me, that the phrase is one in common use and I may easily be deceived; for many a man there is who in flattery says, even to strangers: 'I am quite at your service, I, and whatsoever I have.' And such men are more mocking than jays. So I know not what to think; for it might well be that thus he spake to flatter me. But I saw him change colour and weep right piteously. To my mind his tears, his shamefaced and cast-down countenance, did not come from deceit; no deceit or trickery was there. The eyes from which I saw the tears fall did not lie to me. Signs enow could I see there of love if I know aught of the matter. Yea! I grant that evil was the hour in which I thought it. Evil was the hour that I learnt it, and stored it in my heart; for a very great misfortune has happed to me from it. A misfortune? Truly, by my faith! I am dead, since I see not him who has flattered and cajoled me so much that he has robbed me of my heart. Through his deceit and smooth words, my heart is quitting its lodging and will not stay with me, so much it hates my dwelling and my manor. Faith! then, he who has my heart in his keeping has dealt ill with me. He who robs me and takes away what is mine, loves me not; I know it well. I know it? Why then did he weep? Why? It was not for nothing, for he had reason enow. I ought to apply nought of it to myself because a man's sorrow is very great at parting from those whom he loves and knows. I marvel not that he had grief and sorrow, and that he wept when he left his acquaintances. But he who gave him this counsel to go and stay in Britain could have found no better means of wounding me to the heart. One who loses his heart is wounded to the heart. He who deserves sorrow ought to have it; but I never deserved it. Alas! Unhappy that I am! Why, then, has Cliges slain me without any fault of mine? But in vain do I reproach him; for I have no grounds for this reproach. Cliges would never, never, have forsaken me—I know this well— if his heart had been in like case with mine. In like case I think it is not. And if my heart has joined itself to his heart, never will it leave it, never will his go whither without mine; for mine follows him in secret so close is the comradeship that they have formed. But to tell the truth the two hearts are very different and contrary. How are they different and contrary? His is lord, and mine is slave; and the slave, even against his own will, must do what is for his lord's good and leave out of sight all else. But what matters it to me? He cares nought for my heart or for my service. This division grieves me much; for thus the one heart is lord of the two. Why cannot mine, all alone, avail as much as his with him? Thus the two would have been of equal strength. My heart is a prisoner; for it cannot move unless his moves. And if his wanders or tarries, mine ever prepares to follow and go after him. God! Why are not our bodies so near that I could in some way have fetched my heart back? Have fetched it back? Poor fool! If I were to take it from where it is lodged so comfortably, I might kill it by so doing. Let it stay there. Never do I seek to remove it; rather do I will that it stay with its lord until pity for it come to him; for rather there than here will he be bound to have mercy on his servant because the two hearts are in a strange land. If my heart knows how to serve up flattery as one is bound to serve it up at court, it will be rich before it returns. He who wishes to be on good terms with his lord and to sit beside him on his right, as is now the use and custom, must feign to pluck the feather from his lord's head, even when there is no feather there. But here we see an evil trait: when he flatters him to his face, and yet his lord has in his heart either baseness or villainy, never will he be so courteous as to tell him the truth; rather he makes him think and believe that no one could be a match for him in prowess or in knowledge; and the lord thinks that the courtier is telling the truth. He who believes another anent some quality which he does not possess knows himself ill; for even if he is faithless and stubborn, base and as cowardly as a hare, niggardly and foolish and malformed, worthless in deeds and in words, yet many a man who mocks at him behind his back, extols and praises him to his face; thus then the courtier praises him in his hearing when he speaks of him to another; and yet he pretends that the lord does not hear what they are speaking about together, whereas if he really thought that the lord did not hear, he would never say aught whereat his master would rejoice. And if his lord wishes to lie, he is quite ready with his assent; and whatever his lord says, he asserts to be true; never will he who associates with courts and lords be tongue-tied; his tongue must serve them with falsehood. My heart must needs do likewise if it wishes to have grace of its lord; let it be a flatterer and cajoler. But Cliges is such a brave knight, so handsome, so noble, and so loyal, that never will my heart be lying or false, however much it may praise him; for in him is nothing that can be mended. Therefore, I will that my heart serve him; for the peasant says in his proverb: 'He who commends himself to a good man is base if he does not become better in his service'." Thus Love works on Fenice. But this torment is delight to her, for she cannot be wearied by it.

And Cliges has crossed the sea and has come to Wallingford. There he has demeaned himself in lordly fashion in a fine lodging at a great cost, but he thinks ever of Fenice; never does he forget her for an hour. In the place where he sojourns and tarries, his retinue, as he had commanded, have inquired and questioned persistently till they heard told and related that the barons of King Arthur and the king, himself, in person, had set on foot a tournament in the plains before Oxford which is near Wallingford. In such wise was the joust arranged that it was to last four days. But Cliges will be able to take time to arm his body if he lacks anything meanwhile; for there were more than fifteen whole days to the tournament. He speedily sends three of his squires to London, and bids them buy three different sets of armour: one black, another red, the third green; and as they return he bids that each set of arms be covered with new canvas, so that if anyone meets them on the way he may not know what will be the hue of the arms which they will bring. The squires now set out, 90 to London, and find ready all such equipment as they seek. Soon had they finished, soon did they return; they have come back as soon as they could. They show to Cliges the arms that they had brought; and he praises them much. With these that the emperor gave him on the Danube when he dubbed him knight, he has them stored away and hidden. If anyone now were to ask me why he had them stored away, I would not answer him; for in due time it will be told and related to you, when all the high barons of the land who will come there to gain fame will be mounted on their steeds. On the day that was devised and appointed, the barons of renown assemble. King Arthur, together with the lords whom he had chosen from out the good knights, lay before Oxford. Towards Wallingford went the greater part of his chivalry. Think not that I tell you in order to spin out my tale: such and such kings were there, such and such counts, and such and such others. When the barons were to meet, a knight of great prowess of King Arthur's peers rode out all alone between the two ranks to begin the tourney, as was the custom at that time. But none dares ride forward to come and joust against him. There is none who does not stay where he is; and yet there are some who ask: "Why do these knights wait? Why does none ride forth from the ranks? Surely someone will straightway begin." And on the other side they say: "See ye not what a champion our adversaries have sent us from their side? Let him who has not yet known it know that, of the four bravest known, this is a pillar equal to the rest." "Who is he, then?" "See ye him not? It is Sagremors the Lawless." "Is it he?" "Truly, without doubt." Cliges, who hears and hearkens to this, sat on Morel, and had armour blacker than a ripe mulberry: his whole armour was black. He separates himself from the others in the rank and spurs Morel who comes out of the row; not one is there who sees him but says to his neighbour: "This man rides well with feutred lance; here have we a very skilful knight; he bears his arms in the right fashion; well does the shield at his neck become him. But one cannot but hold him mad as regards the joust he has undertaken of his own accord against one of the bravest known in all this land. But who is he? Of what land is he a native? Who knows him?" "Not I!" "Nor I!" "But no snow has fallen on him! Rather is his armour blacker than monk's or priest's cape." Thus they engage in gossip; and the two champions let their horses go; for no longer do they delay because right eager and aflame are they for the encounter and the shock. Cliges strikes so that he presses Sagremors' shield to his arm, and his arm to his body. Sagremors falls at full length; Cliges acts irreproachably, and makes him declare himself prisoner: Sagremors gives his parole. Now the fight begins, and they charge in rivalry. Cliges has rushed to the combat, and goes seeking joust and encounter. He encounters no knight whom he does not take or lay low. On both sides he wins the highest distinction; for where he rides to joust, he brings the whole tourney to a standstill. Yet he who gallops up to joust with him is not without great prowess; but he wins more renown for standing his ground against Cliges than for taking prisoner another knight; and if Cliges leads him away captive, yet he enjoys great distinction for merely daring to withstand him in the joust. Cliges has the praise and distinction of the whole tournament. And even secretly he has returned to his lodging so that none of them might accost him about one thing or another. And in case any one should have search made for the lodging marked by the black arms, he locks them up in a room so that they may neither be found nor seen; and he has the green arms openly displayed at the door, fronting the road so that the passers by shall see them. And if any asks for him and seeks him, he will not know where his lodging will be, since he will see no sign of the black shield that he seeks. Thus Cliges is in the town and hides himself by such a device. And those who were his prisoners went from end to end of the town asking for the black knight; but none could tell them where he was. And even King Arthur sends up and down to seek him; but all say: "We did not see him after we left the tourney and know not what became of him." More than twenty youths whom the king has sent seek him; but Cliges has so utterly blotted out his tracks that they find no sign of him. King Arthur crosses himself when it was recounted and told him, that neither great nor small is found who can point out his dwelling any more than if he were at Qesarea, or at Toledo, or in Candia. "Faith!" quoth he, "I know not what to say in the matter, but I marvel greatly thereat. It was perhaps a ghost that has moved among us. Many a knight has he overthrown today; and he bears away the parole of the noblest men who will not this year see home or land or country; and each of whom will have broken his oath." Thus the king spake his pleasure though he might very well have kept silence in the matter.

Much have all the barons spoken that night of the black knight, for they spoke of nought else. On the morrow they returned to arms, all without summons and without entreaty. Lancelot of the Lake has dashed forth to make the first joust; for no coward is he; with upright lance he awaits the joust. Lo! Cliges, greener than meadow grass, galloping on a dun, long-maned steed. Where Cliges pricks on the tawny steed, there is none, whether decked with youth's luxuriant locks or bald, who does not behold him with wonder; and they say on both sides: "This man is in all respects much nobler and more skilful than he of yesterday with the black arms, just as the pine is fairer than the beech, and the laurel than the elder. But not yet have we learned who he of yesterday was; but we will learn this very day who this one is. If anyone know it, let him tell us." Each said: "I know him not, never did I see him before to my thinking. But he is fairer than the knight of yesterday and fairer than Lancelot of the Lake. If he were arrayed in a sack and Lancelot in silver and gold, yet this man would still be fairer." Thus all side with Cliges; and the two prick their steeds as fast as they can spur and encounter one another. Cliges proceeds to deal such a blow on the golden shield with the painted lion, that he hurls its bearer from the saddle and fell on him in order to receive his submission. Lancelot could not defend himself and has given his parole. Then the noise and the din and the crash of lances has begun. Those who were on Cliges' side have all their trust in him; for he whom he strikes after due challenge given will never be so strong but that he must needs fall from his horse to the ground. Cliges, this day, wrought so bravely, and threw down and captured so many, that he has pleased those on his side twice as much, and has had twice as much praise from them as he had the day before. When evening has come he has repaired to his lodging as quickly as he could; and speedily bids the red shield and the other armour be brought forth. He orders that the arms which he bore that day be stowed away; the landlord has carefully done it. Long have the knights whom he had captured sought him that night Again; but no news do they hear of him. The greater part of those who speak of him at the inns laud and praise him.

Next day the knights return to arms, alert and strong. From the array before Oxford rides out a knight of great renown; Percival the Welshman, was he called. As soon as Cliges saw him ride forth and heard the truth as to his name—for he heard him called Percival—he greatly longs to encounter him. Forthwith has he ridden forth from the rank on a sorrel, Spanish steed; and his armour was red. Then they, one and all, regard him with great wonder, more than they ever did before and say that never before did they see so comely a knight. And the two prick forward at once; for there was no delay. And the one and the other spurs on so that they give and take mighty blows on their shields. The lances, which were short and thick, bend and curve. In the sight of all who were looking on, Cliges has struck Percival, so that he smites him down from his horse, and makes him give parole without much fighting, and without great ado. When Percival had submitted, then they have begun the tourney; and they all encounter together. Cliges encounters no knight but he fells him to the ground. On this day one could not see him a single hour absent from the fight. Each for himself strikes a blow at Cliges as though at a tower: not merely two or three strike, for then that was not the use or custom. Cliges has made an anvil of his shield; for all play the smith and hammer upon it and cleave and quarter it; but none strikes upon it but Cliges pays him back, and throws him from his stirrups and saddle; and no one, except a man who wished to lie, could have said on his departure that the knight with the red shield had not won that whole day. And the best and most courteous would fain have his acquaintances, but that cannot be so soon; for he has gone away, secretly, when he saw that the sun had set; and he has had his red shield and all his other armour taken away; and he has the white arms brought in which he had been newly knighted; and the arms and the steed were placed in front of the door. But now they begin to perceive (for the greater part who speak of it say so, and perceive it to be so), that they have all been discomfited, and put to flight by a single man, who each day changes his outward show, both horse and armour, and seems another than himself; they have now for the first time perceived it. And my lord Gawain has said that never before did he see such a jouster; and because he would fain have his acquaintance and know his name, he says that he will be first tomorrow at the encounter of the knights. But he makes no boast; rather he says that he thinks and believes that Cliges will have the best of it and will win the renown when they strike with lances; but with the sword, perhaps, Cliges will not be his master; for never could Gawain find his master. Now will he prove himself tomorrow on the strange knight, who every day dons different armour and changes horse and harness. Soon he will be a bird of many moltings if thus daily he makes a practice of taking off his old feathers and putting on new ones. And thus Gawain too doffed his armour, and put on other, and the morrow he sees Cliges return, whiter than lily-flower, his shield held by the straps behind it, on his trusty, white, Arab steed, as he had devised the night before. Gawain, the valiant, the renowned, has not gone to sleep on the field; but pricks, and spurs, and advances, and puts forth all his utmost efforts to joust well if he finds any with whom to joust. Soon both will be on the field for Cliges had no wish to delay; for he had heard the murmur of those who say: "It is Gawain who is no weakling, afoot or on horseback. It is he with whom none dares to measure himself." Cliges, who hears the words, charges into the middle of the field towards him; both advance and encounter with a spring more swift than that of a stag who hears the baying of dogs barking after him. The lances strike on the shields; and so mighty is the crash of the blows, that to their very ends they shatter into splinters, and split, and go to pieces; and the saddle-bows behind, break; moreover, the saddle-girth and breast harness burst. They both alike fall to the ground and have drawn their naked swords. The folk have pressed round to behold the battle. King Arthur came in front of all to separate and reconcile them; but they had broken and hewn in pieces the white hauberks, and had cleft through and cut up the shields, and had fractured the helmets before there was any talk of peace.

The king had gazed at them as long a time as it pleased him; and so did many of the others who said that they esteemed the white knight no whit less in arms than my lord Gawain; and up till now they could not say which was the better, which the worse, nor which would overcome the other if they were allowed to fight till the battle was fought out. But it does not please or suit the king that they do more than they have done. He advances to part them and says to them: "Withdraw! If another blow be struck, it will be to your harm. But make peace. Be friends. Fair nephew Gawain, I entreat you; for it does not become a valiant man to continue a battle or fight where he has no quarrel or hatred. But if this knight would come to my court to pass his time with us, it would be no grievance or hurt to him. Pray him to do so, nephew." "Willingly, Sire." Cliges seeks not to excuse himself from this; willingly he consents to go thither when the tourney shall end; for now he has carried out to the uttermost his father's command. And the king says that he cares not for a tournament which lasts long; well may they straightway leave it. The knights have dispersed, for the king wishes and commands it. Cliges sends for all his armour, for it behoves him to follow the king. With all speed he may have, he comes to the court; but he was attired well beforehand and garbed after the French fashion.

As soon as he came to court each hastens to meet him, for neither one nor the other remains behind; rather they manifest the greatest possible joy and festivity. And all those whom he had taken in the jousting acclaim him lord; but it is his wish to disclaim it to all of them; and he says, that if they think and believe that it was he who took them, they are all absolved of their pledge. There is not a single one who did not say: "It was you, well we know it. We prize highly your acquaintance, and much ought we to love you, and esteem you, and acclaim you, lord, for none of us is a match for you. Just as the sun puts out the little stars, so that their light is not visible in the clouds where the rays of the sun shine forth, so our deeds pale and wane before yours; and yet our deeds were wont to be greatly renowned throughout the world." Cliges knows not what reply to make to them; for it seems to him that one and all of them praise him more than they ought. Though it is very pleasant to him yet he is ashamed of it. The blood rises into his face, so that they see him all ashamed. They escort him through the hall, and have led him before the king; but they all cease to address to him the language of praise and flattery. Now was it the set hour for eating, and those whose business it was, hastened to set the tables. They have set the tables in the palace: some have taken napkins, and others hold basins and give water to those who come. All have washed; all are seated. The king has taken Cliges by the hand and set him before him; for fain will he know this very day who he is, if at all he may. No need is there to speak of the food, for the dishes were as plentiful as though one could have purchased an ox for a farthing.

When all had had their meat and drink, then has the king no longer kept silence. "Friend," quoth he, "I would know if it is from pride that you forbore and disdained to come to my court as soon as you entered this land, and why you thus withdraw yourself from folk and change your arms. Now impart to me your name, and say of what race you are born." Cliges replies: "Never shall it be concealed." He has told and related to the king whatsoever he demands from him; and when the king has learned his name then he embraces him; then he rejoices over him; there is none who does not greet him in clue form. And my Lord Gawain knew him, who, above all, embraces and greets him. All greet him and fall on his neck; and all those who speak of him say that he is right fair and valiant. The king loves him and honours him more than any of all his nephews.

Cliges stays with the king until the beginning of summer; by that time he has been over all Britain and over France and over Normandy, and has wrought many a knightly deed, so that he has well proved himself. But the love with which he is wounded grows neither lighter nor easier. The wish of his heart keeps him ever constant to one thought: he remembers Fenice who far from him is torturing her heart. A longing seizes him to return home; for too long has he abstained from seeing the lady more yearned for than any lady, that ever heard of man has yearned for. And he will not abstain longer from her. He prepares for the journey to Greece; he has taken leave and returns. Much, I ween, did it grieve my lord Gawain and the king when they can no longer keep him. But he longs to reach her whom he loves and desires; and he hastens o'er sea and land; and the way seems very long to him, so eagerly does he yearn to see her who takes away and purloins his heart from him. But she yields him a fair return; and well does she pay and compensate him for the toll she has extorted from him; for she in her turn gives her own heart in payment to him, whom she loves no less. But he is not a whit certain about it; never had he pledge or promise in the matter; and he grieves cruelly. And she also laments; for her love of him is tormenting and killing her; and nothing can give pleasure or joy in her eyes since that hour when she ceased to see him. She does not even know if he is alive, whereof great sorrow strikes her to the heart. But Cliges gets nearer each day, and in his journey he has had good luck; for he has had a fair wind and calm weather, and has anchored with joy and delight before Constantinople. The news reached the city; it was welcome to the emperor and a hundred times more welcome to the empress. If anyone doubt this it will be to his own sorrow. Cliges and his company have repaired to Greece, straight to the port of Constantinople. All the most powerful and noble come to the port to meet him. And when the emperor who had advanced in front of all meets him, and the empress who walks by his side, the emperor, before all, runs to fall on his neck and to greet him. And when Fenice greets him, the one changes colour because of the other; and the marvel is how when they come close to each other they keep from embracing and kissing each other with such kisses as please Love. But folly would it have been and madness. The folk run up in all directions and delight to see him. They all lead him through the midst of the town, some on foot and some on horseback, as far as the imperial palace. Of the joy that there was made will never word here be told, nor of the honour, nor of the homage; but each has striven to do whatever he thinks and believes will please Cliges and be welcome to him. And his uncle yields to him all that he has save the crown. He is right willing that Cliges take at his pleasure whatsoever he shall wish to obtain from him, be it land or treasure; but Cliges makes no account of silver or of gold, since he dare not disclose his thought to her for whom he loses his rest; and yet he has leisure and opportunity for telling her if only he were not afraid of being refused; for every day he can see her and sit alone by her side without anyone gainsaying or forbidding; for nobody imagines or thinks evil of it.

A space of time after he had returned, one day he came unattended into the room of her who was not forsooth his enemy, and be well assured that the door was not shut against the meeting. He was close by her side and all the rest had gone away, so that no one was sitting near them who could hear their words. Fenice first of all questioned him about Britain. She asks him concerning the disposition and courtesy of my lord Gawain, and at last she ventures to speak of what she dreaded. She asked him if he loved dame or maiden in that land. To this Cliges was not unwilling or slow to reply. Quickly was he able to explain all to her, as soon as she challenged him on the point. "Lady," quoth he, "I was in love while yonder; but I loved none who was of yonder land. In Britain my body was without a heart like bark without timber. When I left Germany, I knew not what became of my heart, save that it went away hither after you. Here was my heart and there my body. I was not absent from Greece, for my heart had gone thither, and to reclaim it have I come back here; but it neither comes nor returns to me, and I cannot bring it back to me, and yet I seek it not and cannot do so. And how have you fared since you have come into this land? What joy have you had here? Do the people, does the land please you? I ought to ask you nothing further save this—whether the land please you." "Formerly it pleased me not; but now there dawns for me a joy and a pleasure that I would not lose, be assured, for Pavia or for Placentia; for I cannot dissever my heart from it, nor shall I ever use force to do so. In me is there nought save the bark, for without my heart I live and have my being. Never was I in Britain, and yet my heart has made I know not what contract in Britain without me." "Lady, when was your heart there? Tell me when it went, at what time and at what season, if it is a matter that you can reasonably tell me or another. Was it there when I was there?" "Yes, but you knew it not. It was there as long as you were there and departed with you." "God! and I neither knew nor saw it there. God! why did I know it not? If I had known it, certainly, lady, I would have borne it good company." "Much would you have comforted me and well would it have become you to do so, for I would have been very gracious to your heart, if it had pleased it to come there where it might have known me to be." "Of a surety, lady, it came to you." "To me? Then it came not into exile, for mine also went to you." "Lady, then are both our hearts here with us as you say; for mine is wholly yours." "Friend, and you on your side have mine, and so we are well matched. And know well that, so may God guard me, never had your uncle share in me, for neither did it please me nor was it permitted to him. Never yet did he know me as Adam knew his wife. Wrongly am I called dame; but I know well that he who calls me dame knows not that I am a maid. Even your uncle knows it not, for he has drunk of the sleeping draught and thinks he is awake when he sleeps, and he deems that he has his joy of me, just as he fain would have it, and just as though I were lying between his arms; but well have I shut him out. Yours is my heart, yours is my body, nor indeed will any one by my example learn to act vilely; for when my heart set itself on you, it gave and promised you my body, so that nobody else shall have a share in it. Love for you so wounded me that never did I think to recover any more than the sea can dry up. If I love you and you love me, never shall you be called Tristram, and never shall I be Iseult, for then the love would not be honourable. But I make you a vow that never shall you have other solace of me than you now have, if you cannot bethink yourself how I may be stolen from your uncle and from his bed, so that he may never find me again, or be able to blame either you or me or have anything he may lay hold of herein. To-night must you bend your attention to the matter and to-morrow you will be able to tell me the best device that you will have thought of, and I also will ponder on the matter. To-morrow, when I shall have risen, come early to speak to me, and each will say his thought, and we will carry out that which we shall consider best."

When Cliges heard her wish, he has granted her all, and says that it shall be right well done. He leaves her blithe, and blithe he goes away, and each lies awake in bed all night and they think with great delight over what seems best to them. The morrow they come again together, as soon as they were risen, and they took counsel in private, as there was need for them to do. First Cliges says and recounts what he had thought of in the night. "Lady," quoth he, "I think and believe that we could not do better than go away to Britain: thither have I devised to take you away. Now take heed that the matter fall not through on your side. For never was Helen received at Troy with such great joy, when Paris had brought her thither, that there will not be yet greater joy felt throughout the whole land of the king, my uncle, anent you and me. And if this please you not well, tell me your thought; for I am ready, whatever come of it, to cleave to your thought." She replies: "And I shall speak it. Never will I go with you thus, for then, when we had gone away, we should be spoken of throughout the world as the blonde Iseult and Tristram are spoken of; but here and there all women and men would blame our happiness. No one would believe or could be expected to believe the actual truth of the matter. Who would believe then as regards your uncle that I have gone off and escaped from him still a maid, but a maid to no purpose? Folk would hold me a light-of-love and a wanton, and you a madman. But it is meet to keep and observe the command of St. Paul, for St. Paul teaches him who does not wish to remain continent to act so wisely that he may never incur outcry nor blame nor reproach. It is well to stop an evil mouth, and this I think I can fully accomplish, if it be not too grievous for you; for if I act as my thought suggests to me, I will pretend to be dead. I will shortly feign sickness, and do you on your side lavish your pains to provide for my tomb. Set your attention and care on this, that both tomb and bier be made in such fashion that I die not there nor suffocate, and let no one perceive you that night when you will be ready to take me away. And you will find me a refuge, such that never any save you may see me; and let no one provide me with anything of which I have need or requirement, save you to whom I grant and give myself. Never in all my life do I seek to be served by any other man. You will be my lord and my servant, good will be to me whatsoever you will do to me, nor shall I ever be lady of the empire, if you be not lord of it. A poor, dark, and sordid place will be to me more splendid than all these halls, when you shall be together with me. If I have you and see you, I shall be lady of all the wealth in the world, and the whole world will be mine. And if the thing is done wisely, never will it be interpreted ill, and none will ever be able to point the finger of scorn at me, for through the whole empire folk will believe that I have rotted in the grave. And Thessala, my nurse, who has brought me up and in whom I have great trust, will aid me in good faith, for she is very wise and I have great confidence in her." And Cliges, when he heard his love, replies: "Lady, if so it can be, and if you think that your nurse is likely to counsel you rightly in the matter, all you have to do is to make preparations and to carry them out speedily; but if we act not wisely, we are lost beyond recovery. In this town there is a craftsman who carves and works in wood wondrous well; there is no land where he is not famed for the works of art that he has made and carved and shaped. John is his name, and he is my serf. No handicraft is there, however peculiar it be, in which anyone could rival him, if John set his mind to it with a will. For compared with him they are all novices like a child at nurse. It is by imitating his works that the inhabitants of Antioch and of Rome have learned to do whatever they can accomplish, and no more loyal man is known. But now will I put him to the test, and if I can find loyalty in him, I will free him and all his heirs, and I will not fail to tell him our plan, if he swears and vows to me that he will aid me loyally therein and will never betray me in this matter." She replies: "Now be it so."

By her leave Cliges came forth from the chamber and departed. And she sends for Thessala, her nurse, whom she had brought from the land where she was born. And Thessila came forthwith, for she neither lingers nor delays: but she knows not why her mistress sends for her. Fenice asks her in private conference what she counsels and what seems good to her. She neither hides nor conceals from Thessala even the smallest part of her thought. "Nurse," says she, "I know well that never a thing that I tell you will afterwards become known through you, for I have proved you right well and have found you very wise. You have done so much for me that I love you. Of all my evils I complain to you, nor do I take counsel elsewhere. You know well why I lie awake and what I think and what I wish. My eyes can see nothing to please me, save one thing, but I shall have from it neither enjoyment nor comfort, if I do not pay very dearly for it beforehand. And yet I have found my mate; for if I desire him, he, on his side, desires me too; if I grieve, he, on his side, grieves with my sorrow and my anguish. Now I must confess to you a thought and a parley, in which we two in solitude have resolved and agreed." Then she has told and related to her that she intends to feign herself ill, and says that she will complain so much that finally she will appear dead, and Cliges will steal her away in the night, and they will be always henceforth together. In no other way, it seems to her, could she continue firm in her resolve. But if she were assured that

Thessala would help her in it, the thing could be done according to her wish; "But too long do joy and good fortune for me delay and tarry." Forthwith her nurse assures her that she will lend all her aid to the enterprise, let her now have neither fear nor dread in regard to aught; and she says she will take so much pains about the matter, as soon as she shall undertake it, that never will there be any man who sees her who will not believe quite surely that her soul is severed from the body, when Thessala shall have given her a drink that will make her cold and wan and pale and stiff, without speech and without breath; and yet she will be quite alive and sound, and will feel neither good nor ill, nor will she suffer any harm during a day and a whole night in the tomb and in the bier.

When Fenice had heard it, thus has she spoken and replied: "Nurse, I put myself in your care, I give you free leave to do what you will with me. I am at your disposal; think for me, and bid the folk here that there be none who does not go away. I am ill and they disturb me." The nurse tells them courteously: "My lords, my lady is unwell and wishes you all to go away, for you speak too much and make too much noise, and noise is bad for her. She will have neither rest nor case as long as you are in this room. Never heretofore that I remember had she illness of which I heard her complain so much, so very great and grievous is her sickness. Depart, and it vex you not." They speedily go, one and all, as soon as Thessala had commanded it. And Cliges has quickly sent for John to his lodging, and has said to him privily: "John, knowest thou what I will say? Thou art my serf, I am thy lord, and I Can give thee or sell thee and take thy body and thy goods as a thing that is my own. But if I could trust thee concerning an affair of mine that I am thinking of, thou wouldst for evermore be free, and likewise the heirs which shall be born of thee." John, who much desires freedom, forthwith replies: "Sir," says he, "there is no thing that I would not do wholly at your will, provided that thereby I might see myself free and my wife and children free. Tell me your will; never will there be anything so grievous that it will be toil or punishment to me, nor will it be any burden to me. And were it not so, yet it will behove me to do it even against my will, and set aside all my own business." "True, John, but it is such a thing that my mouth dare not speak it, unless thou warrant me and swear to me, and unless thou altogether assure me that thou wilt faithfully aid me and will never betray me." "Willingly, Sir," quoth John, "never be doubtful of that. For this I swear you and warrant you that as long as I shall be a living man I will never say aught that I think will grieve or vex you." "Ah, John! not even on pain of death is there a man to whom I should dare to say that concerning which I wish to seek counsel of thee; rather would I let my eyes be plucked out. Rather would I that thou shouldst kill me than that thou shouldst say it to any other man. But I find thee so loyal and prudent, that I will tell thee what is in my heart. Thou wilt accomplish my pleasure well, as I think, as regards both thy aid and thy silence." "Truly, Sir! so aid me God!" Forthwith Cliges relates to him and tells him the enterprise quite openly. And when he has disclosed to him the truth, as ye know it who have heard me tell it, then John says that he promises him to make the tomb well and put therein his best endeavour, and says that he will take him to see a house of his own building, and he will show him this that he has made, which never any man, woman, or child yet saw, if it pleases him to go with him there where he is working and painting and carving all by himself without any other folk. He will show him the fairest and most beautiful place that he ever saw. Cliges replies: "Let us then go."

Below the town in a sequestered spot had John built a tower, and he had toiled with great wisdom. Thither has he led Cliges with him, and leads him over the rooms, which were adorned with images fair and finely painted. He shows him the rooms and the fireplaces, and leads him up and down. Cliges sees the house to be lonely, for no one stays or dwells there. He passes from one room to another till he thinks to have seen all, and the tower has pleased him well, and he said that it was very beautiful. The lady will be safe there all the days that she will live; for no man will ever know her to be there. "No, truly, lord, she will never be known to be here. But think you to have seen all my tower and all my pleasaunce? Still are there lurking-places such as no man would be able to find. And if it is allowed you to try your skill in searching as well as you can, never will you be able to ransack so thoroughly as to find more rooms here, however subtle and wise you are, if I do not show and point them out to you. Know that here baths are not lacking, nor anything that I remember and think of as suitable for a lady. She will be well at her ease here. This tower has a wider base underground, as you shall see, and never will you be able to find anywhere door or entrance. With such craft and such art is the door made of hard stone that never will you find the join thereof." "Now hear I marvel," quoth Cliges; "go forward; I shall follow, for I long to see all this." Then has John started off, and leads Cliges by the hand to a smooth and polished door, which is all painted and coloured. At the wall has John stopped, and he held Cliges by the right hand. "Lord," quoth he, "no man is there who could have seen door or window in this wall, and think you that one could pass it in any wise without doing it injury and harm?" Cliges answers that he does not think he could, nor ever will think it, unless he sees it with his own eyes. Then says John that his lord shall see it, for he will open for him the door of the wall. John, who himself had wrought the work, unlocks and opens to him the door of the wall, so that he neither hurts it nor injures it, and the one passes before the other, and they descend by a spiral staircase to a vaulted room where John wrought at his craft, when it was his pleasure to construct aught. "Lord," quoth he, "here where we are was never one of all the men whom God created save us two; and the place has all that makes for comfort, as you will see in a trice. I advise that your retreat be here, and that your lady-love be hidden in it. Such a lodging is meet for such a guest, for there are rooms and baths and in the baths hot water, which comes through a pipe below the earth. That man who would seek a convenient spot to place and hide his lady would have to go far before he found one so delightful. You will deem it a very fitting refuge when you have been all over it." Then has John shown him all, fair chambers and painted vaults, and he has shown him much of his workmanship, which pleased him mightily. When they had seen the whole tower, then said Cliges: "John, my friend, I free you and your heirs one and all, and I am wholly yours. I desire that my lady be here all alone, and that no one ever know it save me and you and her, and not another soul." John replies: "I thank you. Now we have been here long enough, now we have no more to do, so let us start on the return journey." "You have said well," Cliges replies, "let us depart." Then they turn and have issued forth from the tower. On their return they hear in the town how one tells another in confidence: "You know not the grave news about my lady the empress. May the Holy Spirit give health to the wise and noble lady, for she lies in very great sickness."

When Cliges hears the report, he went to the court at full speed; but neither joy nor pleasure was there; for all were sad and dejected on account of the empress, who feigns herself ill; feigns—for the evil whereof she complains gives her no pain or hurt; she has said to all that as long as the malady whereby her heart and head feel pain holds her so strongly, she will have no man save the emperor or his nephew enter her chamber; for she will not deny herself to them; though if the emperor, her lord, come not, little will it irk her. She must needs risk great suffering and great peril for Cliges' sake, but it weighs on her heart that he comes not; she desires to see naught save him. Cliges will soon be in her presence and stay there till he shall have related to her what he has seen and found. He comes before her and has told her; but he remained there a short time only, for Fenice, in order that people may think that what pleases her annoys her, has said aloud: "Away! Away! You tire me greatly, you weary me much; for I am so oppressed with sickness that never shall I be raised from it and restored to health." Cliges, whom this greatly pleases, goes away, making a doleful countenance—for never before did you see it so doleful. Outwardly he appears full sad; but his heart is blithe within, for it looks to have its joy.

The empress, without having any illness, complains and feigns herself ill; and the emperor, who believes her, ceases not to make lamentation, and sends to seek leeches for her; but she will not let that one see her, nor does she let herself be touched. This grieves the emperor, for she says that never will she have leech except one, who will know how to give her health quickly, when it shall be his will. He will make her die or live; into his keeping she puts herself for health and for life. They think that she is speaking of God, but a very different meaning has she, for she means none other than Cliges. He is her God, who can give her health and who can make her die.

Thus the empress provides that no leech attend her, and she will not eat or drink, in order the better to deceive the emperor, until she is both pale and wan all over. And her nurse stays near her, who with very wondrous craft sought secretly through all the town, so that no one knew it, until she found a woman sick of a mortal sickness without cure. In order the better to carry out the deception, she went often to visit her and promised her that she would cure her of her ill, and each day she would bring a glass to see her water, till she saw that medicine would no longer be able to aid her and that she would die that very day. She has brought this water and has kept it straitly until the emperor rose. Now she goes before him and says to him: "If you will, sire, send for all your leeches, for my lady, who is suffering from a sore sickness, has passed water and wishes that the leeches see it, but that they come not in her presence." The leeches came into the hall; they see the water very bad and pale, and each says what seems to him the truth, till they all agree together that never will she recover, and will not even see the hour of None, and if she lives so long, then at the latest God will take her soul to himself. This have they murmured secretly. Then the emperor has bidden and conjured them that they tell the truth of the matter. They reply that they have no hope at all of her recovery, and that she cannot pass the hour of None, for before that hour she will have given up the ghost. When the emperor has heard the word, scarcely can he refrain from swooning to the ground, and likewise many a one of the others who heard it. Never did any folk make such mourning as then prevailed through all the palace. I spare you the account of the mourning, and you shall hear what Thessala is about, who mixes and brews the draught. She has mixed and stirred it, for long beforehand she had provided herself with all that she knew was needed for the draught. A little before the hour of None she gives her the draught to drink. As soon as she had drunk it, her sight grew dim, and her face was as pale and white as if she had lost her blood, nor would she have moved hand or foot even if one had flayed her alive; she neither stirs nor says a word, and yet she hearkens to and hears the mourning which the emperor makes, and the wailing with which the hall is full. And o'er all the city the folk wail who weep and say: "God! what a sorrow and a calamity has accursed death dealt us! Greedy death! Covetous death! Death is worse than any she-wolf, for death cannot be sated. Never couldst thou give a worse wound to the world. Death, what hast thou done? May God confound thee who hast extinguished all beauty. Thou hast slain the choicest creature and the fairest picture—if she had but remained alive!—that God ever laboured to fashion. Too patient is God, since He suffers thee to have the power to ruin His handiwork. Now should God be wroth with thee and cast thee forth from thy dominion, for thou hast committed too wanton and great arrogance and great insult." Thus all the people storm, they wring their hands and beat their palms, and the clerks read there their psalms, who pray for the good lady that God may show mercy to her soul.

Amid the tears and the wails, as the writings tell us, have come three aged physicians from Salerno, where they had been a long time. They have stopped on account of the great mourning, and ask and inquire the reason of the wails and tears, why folk are thus demented and distressed. And they tell them and reply: "God! Lords, know ye not? At this ought the whole world, each place in turn, to become frenzied together with us, if it knew the great mourning and grief and hurt and the great loss which this day has opened to our ken. God! whence then are you come, since you know not what has happened but now in the city? We will tell you the truth, for we wish to join you with us in the mourning wherewith we mourn. Know you nought of ravenous death, who desires all and covets all and in all places lies in wait for the best, and how great an act of folly he hath to-day committed, as he is wont? God had lit the world with a brilliance, with a light. But Death cannot choose but do what he is wont to do. Ever with his might he blots out the best that he can find. Now doth he will to prove his power, and has taken in one body more worth than he has left in the world. If he had taken the whole world, he could not have done one whit worse, provided that he left alive and sound that prey whom he now leads away. Beauty, courtesy, and knowledge, and whatsoever appertaining to goodness a lady can have, has Death, who has destroyed all good in the person of my lady the empress, snatched from us and cheated us of. Thus hath Death slain us." "Ah, God!" say the leeches, "thou hatest this city, we know it well, for that we came not here a little space ago. If we had come yesterday, Death might have esteemed himself highly, if he had taken aught from us by force." "Lords, my lady would not for aught have allowed that you should have seen her or troubled yourself about her. There were enough and to spare of good leeches, but never did my lady please that one or other of them should see her who could meddle with her illness." "No?" "By my faith, that did she truly not." Then they remembered Solomon, and that his wife hated him so much that she betrayed him under a pretence of death. Perhaps this lady has done the same thing; but if they could by any means succeed in touching her, there is no man born for whose sake they would have lied or would refrain from speaking the whole truth about it, if they can see deceit there. Towards the court they go forthwith, where one would not have heard God thundering, such noise and wailing there was. The master of them, who knew the most, has approached the bier. None says to him: "You touch it at your peril." Nor does any one pull him back from it. And he puts his hand on her breast and on her side and feels beyond a doubt that she has her life whole in her body; well he knows it and well he perceives it. He sees before him the emperor, who is frenzied and ready to kill himself with grief. He cries aloud and says to him: "Emperor, comfort thyself. I know and see for a certainty that this lady is not dead. Leave thy mourning and console thyself. If I give her not back to thee alive, either slay me or hang me." Now all the wailing throughout the palace is calmed and hushed, and the emperor tells the leech that now it is permitted him to give orders and to speak his will quite freely. If he brings back the empress to life, he will be lord and commander over him; but he will be hanged as a robber, if he has lied to him in aught. And he says to him: "I accept the condition; never have mercy on me, if I do not make the lady here speak to you. Without hesitation or delay have the palace cleared for me. Let not one or another stay here. I must see privately the evil from which the lady suffers. These two leeches alone, who are of my company, shall stay here with me, and let all the others go without." This thing Cliges, John, and Thessala would have gainsaid: but all those who were there would have interpreted it to their harm, if they had attempted to prevent it. Therefore they keep silence and give the counsel that they hear the others give, and have gone forth from the palace. And the three leeches have by force ripped up the lady's winding-sheet, for there was neither knife nor scissors: then they say: "Lady, have no fear, be not dismayed, but speak in all safety. We know for a surety that you are quite sound and well. Now be wise and amenable, and despair of nought; for if you seek advice from us, we will assure you all three of us, that we will help you with all our power, where it be concerning good or concerning evil. We will be right loyal towards you, both in keeping your secret and in aiding you. Do not compel us to reason long with you. From the moment that we place our power and services at your disposal, you ought not to refuse us compliance." Thus they think to befool and to cheat her, but it avails nought; for she cares and recks nought of their service, so that when the physicians see that they will avail nothing with regard to her by cajolery or by entreaty, then they take her off the bier and strike her and beat her; but their fury is to no purpose, since for all this they draw not a word from her. Then they threaten and frighten her and say that, if she does not speak, she will that very day find out the folly of her action; for they will inflict on her such dire treatment that never before was its like inflicted on any body of caitiff woman. "Well we know that you are alive and do not deign to speak to us. Well we know that you are feigning and would have deceived the emperor. Have no fear of us at all. But if any man has angered you, disclose your folly, before we have further wounded you, for you are acting very basely; and we will aid you, alike in wisdom or in folly." It cannot be, it avails them nought. Then once more they deal her blows on the back with their straps, and the stripes that run downwards become visible, and so much do they beat her tender flesh that they make the blood gush out from it. When they have beaten her with straps till they have lacerated her flesh, and till the blood which issues through her wounds runs down from them, and when for all that they can do nothing nor extort sigh or word promise her; they are meddling to no purpose. And from her, and she never moves nor stirs, then they tell her that they must seek fire and lead, and that they will melt it and will pour it into her palms rather than fail to make her speak. They seek and search for fire and lead; they kindle the fire; they melt the lead. Thus the base villains maltreat and torture the lady, for they have poured into her palms the lead, all boiling and hot just as they have taken it from the fire. Nor yet is it enough for them that the lead has passed through and through the palms, but the reprobate villains say that, if she speak not soon, straightway they will roast her till she is all grilled. She is silent and forbids them not to beat or ill-treat her flesh. And even now they were about to put her to the fire to roast and grill, when more than a thousand of the ladies, who were in front of the palace, come to the door and see through a tiny chink the torture and the unhappy fate that they were preparing for the lady, for they were making her suffer martyrdom from the coal and from the flame. To break in the door and shatter it they bring hatchets and hammers. Great was the din and the attack to break and smash the door. If now they can lay hold on the leeches, without delay all their desert shall be rendered them. The ladies enter the palace all together with one bound, and Thessala is among the press, whose one anxiety is to get to her lady. She finds her all naked at the fire, much injured and much mishandled. She has laid her back on the bier and covered her beneath the pall. And the ladies proceed to tender and pay to the three leeches their deserts; they would not send for or await emperor or seneschal. They have hurled them down through the windows full into the court, so that they have broken the necks and ribs and arms and legs of all three; better never wrought any ladies. Now the three leeches have received from the ladies right sorry payment for their deeds; but Cliges is much dismayed and has great grief, when he hears tell of the great agony and the torture that his lady has suffered for him. Almost does he lose his reason; for he fears greatly and indeed with justice—that she may be killed or maimed by the torture caused her by the three leeches, who have died in consequence; and he is despairing and disconsolate. And Thessala comes bringing a very precious salve with which she has anointed full gently the lady's body and wounds. The ladies have enshrouded her again in a white Syrian pall, wherein they had shrouded her before, but they leave her face uncovered. Never that night do they abate their wailing or cease or make an end thereof. Through all the town they wail like folk demented-high and low, and poor and rich-and it seems that each sets his will on outdoing all the others in making lamentation, and on never abandoning it of his own will. All night is the mourning very great. On the morrow John came to court, and the emperor sends for him and bids him, requests and commands him: "John! if ever thou madest a good work, now set all thy wisdom and thy invention to making a tomb, such that one cannot find one so fair and well decorated." And John, who had already done it, says that he has prepared a very fair and well-carved one; but never, when he began to make it, had he intention that any body should be laid there save a holy one. "Now, let the empress be enclosed within in lieu of relics; for she is, I ween, a very holy thing." "Well said," quoth the emperor, "in the minster of my lord Saint Peter shall she be buried, there outside where one buries other bodies; for before she died, she begged and prayed me with all her heart that I would have her laid there. Now go and busy yourself about it, and set your tomb, as is right and meet, in the fairest place in the cemetery." John replies: "Gladly, sire." Forthwith John departs, prepares well the tomb, and did thereat what a master of his craft would do. Because the stone was hard, and even more on account of the cold, he has placed therein a feather bed; and moreover, that it may smell sweet to her, he has strewn thereon both flowers and foliage. But he did it even more for this, that none should spy the mattress that he had placed in the grave. Now had the whole office been said in chapels and in parish churches, and they were continually tolling as it is meet to toll for the dead. They bid the body be brought, and it will be placed in the tomb, whereat John has worked to such effect that he has made it very magnificent and splendid. In all Constantinople has been left neither great nor small who does not follow the corpse weeping, and they curse and revile Death; knights and squires swoon, and the dames and the maidens beat their breasts and have railed against Death. "Death!" quoth each, "why took'st thou not a ransom for my lady? Forsooth, but a small booty hast thou gained, and for us the loss is great." And Cliges, of a truth, mourns so much that he wounds and maltreats himself more than all the others do, and it is a marvel that he does not kill himself; but still he postpones suicide till the hour and the time come for him to disinter her and hold her in his arms, and know whether she is alive or not. About the grave are the lords, who lay the body there; but they do not meddle with John in the setting up of the tomb, and indeed they could see nought of it, but have all fallen swooning to the earth, and John has had good leisure to do all he listed. He so set up the tomb that there was no other creature in it; well does he seal and join and close it. Then might that man well have boasted himself who, without harm or injury, would have been able to take away or disjoin aught that John had put there.

Fenice is in the tomb, until it came to dark night; but thirty knights guard her, and there are ten tapers burning, and they made a great light. The knights were sated and weary with mourning, and have eaten and drunk in the night till they all lay asleep together. At night Cliges steals forth from the court and from all the folk. There was not knight or servant who ever knew what had become of him. He did not rest till he came to John, who gives him all the counsel that he can. He puts on him a suit of armour, which he will never need. Both all armed go forth to the cemetery at post haste; but the cemetery was enclosed all around by a high wall; and the knights, who were sleeping, and had closed the door within that none might enter, thought they were safe. Cliges sees not how he may pass, for he cannot enter by the door, and yet by hook or by crook he must enter, for love exhorts and admonishes him. He grips the wall and mounts up, for right strong and agile was he. Within was an orchard and there were trees in plenty. Near the wall one had been planted so that it touched the wall. Now has Cliges what he wished for; he let himself down by this tree. The first thing that he did was to go and open the door to John. They see the knights sleeping and they have extinguished all the tapers, so that no light remains there. And now John uncovers the grave and opens the tomb, so that he injures it not at all. Cliges leaps into the grave and has carried forth his lady, who is very weak and lifeless, and he falls on her neck and kisses and embraces her. He knows not whether to rejoice or mourn; for she moves not nor stirs. And John has closed again the tomb with all the speed he may, so that it does not in any wise appear that it had been touched. They have approached the tower as quickly as ever they could. When they had put her within the tower in the rooms that were underground, then they took off the grave-clothes, and Cliges, who knew nothing of the draught that she had within her body, which makes her dumb and prevents her stirring, thinks in consequence that she is dead, and he loses hope and comfort thereat, and sighs deeply and weeps. But soon the hour will have come that the draught will lose its force. And Fenice, who hears him lament, tries and strains that she may be able to comfort him either by word or by look. Her heart nearly breaks because of the mourning she hears him make. "Ha! Death," quoth he, "how base thou art, in that thou sparest and passest by worthless and outcast creatures! Such thou dost allow to last and live. Death! art thou mad or drunk that thou has killed my love without killing me? This that I see is a marvel: my love is dead and I am alive. Ah, sweet love! why does your lover live and see you dead? Now might one rightly say that you are dead for my sake, and that I have killed and slain you. Loved lady! then am I the Death who has killed you; is not that unjust? For I have taken away my life in you and yet have kept yours in me. For were not your health and your life mine, sweet friend? And were not mine yours? For I loved nought but you: we twain were one being. Now have I done what I ought, for I keep your soul in my body, and mine is gone forth of yours; and yet the one was bound to bear the other company, wherever it was, and nothing ought to have parted them." At this she heaves a sigh and says in a weak, low voice: "Friend! friend! I am not wholly dead, but well-nigh so. But I hope nought about my life. I thought to have a jest and to feign: but now must I needs complain, for Death loves not my jest. A marvel 'twill be if I escape alive, for much have the leeches wounded me, broken and lacerated my flesh; and nevertheless, if it could be that my nurse were here with me, she would make me quite whole, if care could avail aught herein." "Friend! then let it not distress you," quoth Cliges, "for this very night I will bring her here for you.....Friend! rather will John go." John goes thither and has sought till he found her, and he imparts to her how greatly he desires her to come; never let any excuse detain her; for Fenice and Cliges summon her to a tower where they await her; for Fenice is sore mishandled, and she must come provided with salves and electuaries, and let her know that the lady will live no longer if she succour her not speedily. Thessala forthwith runs and takes ointment and plaster and an electuary that she had made, and has joined company with John. Then they issue from the town secretly and go till they come straight to the tower. When Fenice sees her nurse, she thinks she is quite cured, so much she loves her and believes in her and trusts her. And Cliges embraces and greets her and says: "Welcome, nurse! for I love and esteem you greatly. Nurse, in God's name what think you of this damsel's illness? What is your opinion? Will she recover?" "Ay, sir! fear not that I cannot cure her right well. A fortnight will not have passed before I make her whole, so that never at any time was she more whole and gay."

Thessala sets her mind on curing the lady, and John goes to provide the tower with whatsoever store is meet. Cliges comes and goes to the tower boldly, in view of all, for he has left there a goshawk moulting, and says that he comes to see it, and none can guess that he goes there for any other reason save only on account of the hawk. Much does he tarry there both night and day. He makes John guard the tower, that no one may enter there against his will. Fenice has no hurt whereof she need grieve, for well has Thessala cured her. If now Cliges had been duke of Almeria or of Morocco or of Tudela, he would not have prized such honour a berry in comparison of the joy he has. Certes, Love abased himself no whit when he put them together; for it seems to both when one embraces and kisses the other that the whole world is made better for their joy and their pleasure. Ask me no more about it; I will but say that there is nought that one wills that the other does not welcome. So is their will at one as if they twain were but one. All this year and some space of the next, two months and more, I ween, has Fenice been in the tower, until the spring of the year. When flowers and foliage bud forth, and the little birds are making merry—for they delight in their bird-language—it happened that Fenice heard one morning the nightingale sing. Cliges was holding her gently with one arm about her waist and the other about her neck, and she him in like manner, and she has said to him: "Fair, dear friend, much joy would an orchard afford me, where I could take my pleasure. I have seen neither moon nor sun shine for more than fifteen whole months. If it might be, full gladly would I sally forth into the daylight, for I am pent up in this tower. If near by there were an orchard where I could go to disport myself, great good would this do me often." Then Cliges promises that he will seek counsel of John as soon as he shall see him. And now it has happened that lo! John has come thither, for he was often wont to come. Cliges has spoken with him of Fenice's desire. "All is prepared and already at hand," quoth John, "whatsoever she orders. This tower is well provided with all that she wishes and asks for." Then is Fenice right blithe and bids John lead her thither, and John makes no demur. Then goes John to open a door, such that I have neither skill nor power to tell or describe the fashion of it. None save John could have had the skill to make it, nor could any one ever have told that there was door or window there, as long as the door was not opened, so hidden and concealed was it.

When Fenice saw the door open and the sun which she had not seen for a long time shine in, she has all her blood awhirl with joy and says that now she seeks nothing more, inasmuch as she can come forth out of the hiding-place, and seeks no refuge elsewhere. By the door she has entered the orchard, and this greatly pleases and delights her. In the midst of the orchard there was a grafted tree loaded with flowers and very leafy, and it formed a canopy above. The branches were so trained that they hung towards the ground and bent almost to the earth, all save the top from which they sprang, for that rose straight upwards. Fenice desires no other place. And below the grafted tree the meadow is very delectable and very fair, nor ever will the sun be so high even at noon, when it is hottest, that ever a ray can pass that way, so skilled was John to arrange things and to guide and train the branches. There Fenice goes to disport herself, and all day she makes her couch there; there they are in joy and delight. And the orchard is enclosed around with a high wall which joins the tower, so that no creature could enter it, unless he had climbed to the top of the tower.

Now is Fenice in great delight: there is nought to displease her, nor lacks she aught that she could wish, when 'neath the flowers and leaves it lists her embrace her lover. At the time when folk go hunting with the sparrow-hawk and with the hound, which seeks the lark and the stonechat and tracks the quail and the partridge, it happened that a knight of Thrace, a young and sprightly noble, esteemed for his prowess, had one day gone a-hawking quite close beside this tower; Bertrand was the knight's name. His sparrow-hawk had soared high, for it had missed the lark that was its aim. Now will Bertrand consider himself ill served by fate, if he lose his sparrow-hawk. He saw it descend and settle below the tower in an orchard, and it pleased him much to see this, for now he reckons that he will not lose it. Forthwith he goes to scale the wall, and wins to get over it. Under the grafted tree he saw Fenice and Cliges sleeping together side by side. "God!" quoth he, "what has befallen me? What kind of miracle is it that I see? Is it not Cliges? Yea, faith. Is not that the empress by his side? Nay, but she resembles her, for no other being ever was so like. Such a nose, such a mouth, such a brow she has as the empress, my lady, had. Never did nature better succeed in making two beings of the same countenance. In this lady see I nought that I should not have seen in my lady. If she had been alive, truly I should have said that it was she." At that moment a pear drops and falls just beside Fenice's ear. She starts, awakes, sees Bertrand and cries aloud: "Friend, friend, we are lost! Here is Bertrand! If he escapes you, we have fallen into an evil trap. He will tell folk that he has seen us." Then has Bertrand perceived that it is the empress beyond all doubt. Need is there for him to depart, for Cliges had brought his sword with him into the orchard, and had laid it beside the couch. He springs up and has taken his sword, and Bertrand flees swiftly. With all the speed he might he grips the wall, and now he was all but over it, when Cliges has come after, raises now his sword, and strikes him, so that beneath the knee he has cut off his leg as clean as a stalk of fennel. Nevertheless, Bertrand has escaped ill-handled and crippled, and on the other side he is received by his men, who are beside themselves with grief and wrath, when they see him thus maimed; they have asked and inquired who it is that had done it to him. "Question me not about it," quoth he, "but raise me on my horse. Never will this story be recounted till it is told before the emperor. He who has done this to me ought not forsooth to be without fear—nor is he, for he is nigh to deadly peril." Then they have put him on his palfrey, and, mourning, they lead him away in great dismay through the midst of the town. After them go more than twenty thousand, who follow him to the court. And all the people flock there, the one after the other, and the devil take the hindmost.

Now has Bertrand made his plea and complaint to the emperor in the hearing of all, but they consider him an idle babbler because he says that he has seen the empress stark naked. All the town is stirred thereat; some, when they hear this news, esteem it mere folly, others advise and counsel the emperor to go to the tower. Great is the uproar and the tumult of the folk who set out after him. But they find nothing in the tower, for Fenice and Cliges are on their way, and have taken Thessala with them, who comforts and assures them, and says that, even if perchance they see folk coming after them who come to take them, they need have no fear for aught, for never to do them harm or injury would they come within the distance that one could shoot with a strong crossbow stretched by windlass.

Now the emperor is in the tower and he has John sought out and fetched: he bids that he be tied and bound, and says that he will have him hanged or burned and the ashes scattered to the wind. For the shame that the emperor has suffered, John shall pay the penalty (but it will be a bootless penalty!) because he has secreted in his tower the nephew and the wife of the emperor. "I'faith you speak the truth," quoth John; "I will not lie in the matter; I will stick to the truth throughout, and if I have done wrong in any point, right meet is it that I be taken. But on this score I could well excuse myself, that a serf ought to refuse nought that his rightful lord commands him. And it is known full surely that I am his and the tower is his." "Nay, John, rather is it thine." "Mine, sire? Truly, as his serf I am not even my own, nor have I anything that is mine, save in so far as he grants it to me. And if you would say that my lord has done you wrong, I am ready to defend him from the charge without his bidding me so to do. But the knowledge that I must die makes me bold to speak out freely my will and my mind as I have fashioned and moulded it. Now, be that as it may be, for if I die for my lord, I shall not die in dishonour. Surely without a doubt is known the oath and promise that you pledged to your brother, that after you, Cliges, who is going away into exile, should be emperor. And if it please God, he will yet be emperor. And you are to be blamed for this, for you ought not to have taken wife, but all the same you took one and wronged Cliges, and he has wronged you in nought. And if I am done to death by you and die for him unjustly, if he lives, he will avenge my death. Now do your utmost, for if I die, you will die too."

Beads of wrath break out on the emperor's brow when he has heard the words and the insult that John has uttered against him. "John," quoth he, "thou shalt have respite until what time thy lord be found, for base has he proved himself towards me, who held him right dear, nor thought to defraud him. But thou shalt be kept fast in prison. If thou knowest what has become of him, tell me straightway, I bid thee." "Tell you? And how should I commit so great a treason? Of a surety, I would not betray to you my lord, not though you were to rend my life out of my body, if I knew it. And besides this, so may God be my guard, I cannot say any more than you in what direction they have gone. But you are jealous without a cause. Too little do I fear your wrath not to tell you truly in the hearing of all how you are deceived, and yet I shall never be believed in this matter. By a potion that you drank, you were tricked and deceived the night that you celebrated your wedding. Never at any time, save when you slept and it happened to you in your dreams, did any joy come to you of her; but the night made you dream, and the dream pleased you as much as if it had happened in your waking hours that she held you in her arms; and no other boon came to you from her. Her heart clave so straitly to Cliges that for his sake she pretended to be dead; and he trusted me so much that he told me and placed her in my house, of which he is lord by right. You ought not to lay the blame on me for it; I should have merited to be burnt or hanged, if I had betrayed my lord and refused to do his will."

When the emperor heard tell of the potion which it delighted him to drink, and by which Thessala deceived him, then first he perceived that he had never had joy of his wife—well he knew it—unless it had happened to him in a dream, and that such joy was illusory. He says that, if he take not vengeance for the shame and the disgrace brought on him by the traitor who has carried off from him his wife, never again will he have joy in his life. "Now, quick!" quoth he, "to Pavia, and from there to Germany, let neither castle, town, nor city be left where he be not sought. He who shall bring them both prisoners will be more cherished by me than any other man. Now, set well to work and search both up and down and near and far!" Then they start with great zeal, and they have spent all the day in searching; but Cliges had such friends among them that, if they found the lovers, they rather would lead them to a place of refuge than bring them back. Throughout a whole fortnight with no small pains they have pursued them, but Thessala, who is guiding them, leads them so safely by art and by enchantment that they have no fear or alarm for all the forces of the emperor. In no town or city do they lie, and yet they have whatsoever they wish and desire, as good as or better than they are wont to have, for Thessala seeks and procures and brings for them whatsoever they wish, and no one follows or pursues them, for all have abandoned the quest. But Cliges does not delay; he goes to his uncle, King Arthur. He sought him till he found him, and has made to him a complaint and an outcry against his uncle the emperor, who, in order to disinherit him, had taken wife dishonourably, when he should not have done so, seeing that he had pledged his word to Cliges' father that never in his life would he have a wife. And the king says that with a navy will he sail to Constantinople, and fill a thousand ships with knights and three thousand with infantry, such that nor city nor borough nor town nor castle, however strong or high it be, will be able to endure their onset. And Cliges has not forgotten to thank the king then and there for the aid which he is granting him. The king sends to seek and to summon all the high barons of his land, and has ships and boats, cutters and barques sought out and equipped. With shields, with lances, with targes, and with knightly armour he has a hundred ships filled and laden. The king makes so great a preparation to wage war that never had even Cesar or Alexander the like. He has caused to be summoned and mustered all England and all Flanders, Normandy, France, and Brittany, and all tribes, even as far as the Spanish passes. Now were they about to put to sea when messengers came from Greece, who stayed the expedition and kept back the king and his men. With the messengers who came was John, who was well worthy to be believed, for he was witness and messenger of nought that was not true and that he did not know for certain. The messengers were high men of Greece, who were seeking Cliges. They sought and asked for him until they found him at the court of the king, and they have said to him: "God save you, sire. On the part of all the inhabitants of your empire, Greece is yielded and Constantinople given to you, because of the right that you have to it. Your uncle—as yet you know it not—is dead of the grief that he had because he could not find you. He had such grief that he lost his senses: never afterwards did he either eat or drink, and he died a madman. Fair sire, return now hence, for all your barons send for you. Greatly do they desire and ask for you, for they will to make you emperor." Many there were who were blithe at this message, but on the other hand there were man who would gladly have left their homes, and who would have been mightily pleased if the host had set out for Greece. But the expedition has fallen through altogether, for the king sends away his men, and the host disperses and returns home. But Cliges hastens and prepares himself, for his will is to return into Greece, no care has he to tarry longer. He has prepared himself, and has taken leave of the king and all his friends: he takes Fenice with him, and they depart and do not rest till they are in Greece, where men receive him with great joy, as they ought to do their lord, and give him his lady-love to wife; they crown them both together. He has made his lady-love his wife, but he calls her lady-love and dame, nor does she for that cease to be cherished as his lady-love, and she cherishes him every whit as much as one ought to cherish one's lover. And each day their love grew; never did he mistrust her nor chide her for aught. She was never kept in seclusion, as those who came after her later have been kept (for henceforth there was no emperor who was not afraid lest his wife might deceive him, when he heard tell how Fenice deceived Alis, first by the potion that he drank and then by the other treason). For which reason the empress, whoever she be, be she of never so splendid and high degree, is guarded in Constantinople; for the emperor trusts her not as long as he remembers Fenice.

www.ingramcontent.com/pod-product-compliance
Lightning Source LLC
LaVergne TN
LVHW041736190726
843493LV00008B/2383